WILL I EVER
BE FREE OF YOU?

WILL I EVER
BE FREE OF YOU?

HOW TO NAVIGATE A HIGH-CONFLICT DIVORCE
FROM A NARCISSIST AND HEAL YOUR FAMILY

Karyl McBride, Ph.D.

ATRIA BOOKS

New York   London   Toronto   Sydney   New Delhi

ATRIA BOOKS

A Division of Simon & Schuster, Inc.
1230 Avenue of the Americas
New York, NY 10020

First Atria Books hardcover edition February 2015

ATRIA BOOKS and colophon are trademarks of Simon & Schuster, Inc.

For information about special discounts for bulk purchases,
please contact Simon & Schuster Special Sales at 1-800-456-6798
or business@simonandschuster.com.

The Simon & Schuster Speakers Bureau can bring authors to your live event.
For more information or to book an event contact the Simon & Schuster Speakers
Bureau at 1-866-248-3049 or visit our website at www.simonspeakers.com.

Manufactured in the United States of America

10   9   8   7   6   5

Library of Congress Cataloging-in-Publication Data

McBride, Karyl.
  Will I ever be free of you? : how to navigate a high-conflict divorce from a
narcissist and heal your family / Karyl McBride, Ph.D.
      pages cm
   Includes bibliographical references and index.
   1. Divorce. 2. Marriage. 3. Narcissism. I. Title.
  HQ814.M35 2015
  306.89—dc23
  2014026433

ISBN 978-1-4767-5569-4
ISBN 978-1-4767-5573-1 (ebook)

To my loving children and special grand angels: Nate, Paula, Meggan, David, McKenzie, Isabella, Declan, Cillian, Alex, and Ken.

CONTENTS

CONTENTS

INTRODUCTION

For the past twelve years a yellow sticky note has somehow clung to my refrigerator. It says, "Go After Your Purpose and God Will Give You Your Dream." I stuck that quote on the fridge when I was writing my first book, *Will I Ever Be Good Enough? Healing the Daughters of Narcissistic Mothers*. It's dog-eared and faded, but it still greets me as I begin each day.

The purpose that has driven me throughout my career is the hope that I can help people make sense of the many complications in their lives created by dysfunctional families and guide them in healing from the legacy of distorted love that results. In my thirty-plus years as a therapist, I have seen that narcissism, a personality disorder that goes beyond mere selfishness and vanity, is a prevalent cause of family problems. Narcissists are grandiose in their need for praise and attention. While they often overestimate their own abilities, they diminish the people around them, particularly the ones they claim to love. Being in an intimate relationship with a narcissist can be exhilarating and all-consuming, but often, in the end, the narcissist consumes you, your hopes and dreams, your peace of mind, and your money.

From the clinician's chair, I have heard the pain and seen the tears of narcissists' victims, including adult children, young children, partners and spouses, abused children, and victims of crime. This work has also led me to specialty areas, such as forensic interviewing and expert-witness testimony, and much interaction with the court system, attorneys, judges, law enforcement, and social services, on which I draw to help you in this book.

Many people wrote to me after my first book, *Will I Ever Be Good Enough?*, was published to share their personal stories of life with a narcissistic mother. I was honored to receive so much correspondence from around the world and touched that readers reached out to me. In addition to their relationships with their mothers, however, my readers also wanted to talk about their romantic relationships. In reading the first book, they had learned that their mothers' narcissism had distorted their expectations of love so much that their relationships were now with other narcissists. Their letters described them as trapped in conflicts with narcissistic partners, enduring unending arguments and manipulations, saddled with enormous legal bills and never coming to a resolution. Almost every letter held a tone of despair. Why did they keep falling into partnerships with narcissists? Their questions led me to conduct more research and clinical work, and to write this second book.

As you read on, please know in my heart I wish I were sitting with you on this journey to understanding your life. It is difficult to find yourself in such turmoil and pain, and difficult to comprehend how a relationship that probably started with such a powerful attraction could devolve so completely. Love is the greatest gift we give to each other, but narcissists do not have the capacity to love. They're charmers, especially in the beginning of a relationship, but their limited ability to empathize or sympathize with other people's feelings causes confusion and pain to their partners. It is also devastating to the children they bring into the world.

If you are a child of a narcissistic parent or have fallen into the deep pit of a relationship with a narcissist, then you have probably been prevented from developing a whole and healthy life. I believe that you can free yourself from the pain that narcissists have caused you, learn more about yourself, and heal yourself and help your children heal, too. I hope this book brings you important information that will make a difference for you and your loved ones.

Will I Ever Be Free of You? is divided into three parts: "Recognizing the Problem," "Breaking Free," and "Healing from the Debilitating Impact of Narcissistic Relationships." First the book shows you how to recognize the problems that a narcissistic partner causes you and your children. Then it helps you to understand the confusing dynamics of being involved with a narcissist, to weigh and balance whether you should stay in the relationship or leave, and when to make the right life choices for yourself and your children. And finally it provides you with a road map for recovery. As a divorce will likely involve the judicial system, the book also addresses issues you'll come up against and how to deal with them in the current system. I also present my ideas about needed court reforms.

In this practical guide you will learn how to weigh what is best for you and your children as you deal with a narcissistic partner. Don't try to navigate a divorce on your own. Educate and prepare yourself to understand how narcissists react to disagreement, separation, divorce, and child custody. While I will tell you about some of the bad things that have happened to other people who have been through narcissistic relationships, I'll also tell you the positive side of getting free and about the healthy, healing experiences you can then have. If you recognize yourself or your partner or spouse in these stories you read, I hope you will have the courage to continue and begin your recovery.

Ultimately, the message of this book is one of hope. If you have ever looked at your partner and thought in despair, *Will I ever be free of you?*, the answer is yes, you can be free. This book offers tools to protect and nurture you and your children. Once you understand what turned your life upside down and inside out, you can break free and rediscover your authentic self. You can free yourself and your children from the legacy of distorted love. Let's get started.

PART ONE

RECOGNIZING THE PROBLEM

CHAPTER ONE

Am I in a Relationship with a Narcissist? How Do I Know?

When Ellen entered her first therapy session with me, she held a card in her hand that she'd printed out from Someecards .com. Without speaking, she handed it to me. It read, "We divorced for religious reasons. My partner thought he was God and I didn't." While I smiled at the humor, it gave me a good sense about what she would tell me in her story.

When Mark and Ellen first met, Ellen felt caught up in a whirlwind of excitement. Mark was charming, witty, and seductive. Ellen believed that what she and Mark felt for each other was true love. She didn't realize until after they'd married and had children that Mark's charm was that of an artful narcissist. Despite his initial showy displays of love, Mark cared only about himself and consistently manipulated others to get his own needs met. He emotionally abused Ellen and their children. When Ellen decided that she had had enough and filed for divorce, Mark was appalled. He could not believe that Ellen would abandon him and ruin his life. Mark saw himself as the victim.

Unwilling to compromise, unable to see things from any perspective other than his own, consistently angry and vindictive, Mark created havoc for Ellen through the divorce, lashed out during each phase of the proceedings, and had excuses for even his most egregious behavior, blaming others—especially Ellen—for his actions. He never thought twice about using his children as pawns. The judge got increasingly frustrated as Mark and Ellen showed up in court again and again.

When a divorcing couple is made up of one narcissist and one reasonably normal person, the narcissistic spouse can single-handedly create all kinds of conflict. The narcissist's actions cause the "normal" spouse to go into defense mode—especially when children are involved. To outsiders, it looks like a fight between equals, but what is really happening is that the normal spouse is trying to protect the children from a bully. Many people do not recognize the qualities of narcissism, even when they are involved with a narcissist.

A common perception among divorce lawyers, therapists, parenting-time evaluators, judges, and other professionals is that, whenever you have a "high-conflict" divorce, both parties are responsible for the conflict. Many professionals assume that difficult, drawn-out custody battles are caused by two parents who are each stubborn, selfish, and perhaps a bit crazy. As Michael Friedman wrote in an article for *The American Journal of Family Therapy*, "The concept has even entered into what might be called family court folk wisdom: we say that Mother Teresa does not marry Attila the Hun or that it takes two to tango."[1]

People use the label *narcissist* loosely, typically to indicate someone who is vain and selfish, but the personality disorder is precisely defined and has been studied by mental health professionals who have identified the traits of narcissists. How do you recognize someone who is a narcissist, as opposed to someone who has a healthy self-respect or even someone who is disagreeably arrogant, but not an actual narcissist?

Could This Be My Partner (or My Ex)?

The term *narcissism* comes from the Greek myth of Narcissus, a handsome young man who believed himself to be better and more beautiful than everyone else and who fell in love with his own reflection in a pool of water. Whenever he reached out to capture this vision of beauty, however, he touched the water and shattered the reflection. Even so, he could not tear himself away and lost all interest in food, rest, and normal life. Gradually, he lost the strength and the beauty that had made him so appealing and died while gazing at his reflection. His unhealthy self-love was a curse. Sigmund Freud used this myth to describe a psychological disorder—a disease of self-love—that he saw in some of his clients.[2]

The American Psychiatric Association (APA) classifies mental disorders according to their symptoms in *The Diagnostic and Statistical Manual of Mental Disorders* (*DSM*). The *DSM* includes narcissism with personality disorders that lead to dramatic, emotional, or erratic behavior, such as borderline personality disorder (BPD) and histrionic personality disorder (HPD). These personality disorders have a lot of "comorbidity," meaning that someone can have more than one of them at once. The nine traits listed below from the *DSM* define the narcissistic personality:

1. Has a grandiose sense of self-importance, e.g., exaggerates achievements and talents, and expects to be recognized as superior without commensurate achievements.
2. Is preoccupied with fantasies of unlimited success, power, brilliance, beauty, or ideal love.
3. Believes that he or she is "special" and unique and can only be understood by, or should associate with, other special or high-status people (or institutions).
4. Requires excessive admiration.
5. Has a sense of entitlement, i.e., unreasonable expectations of especially favorable treatment or automatic compliance with his or her expectations.
6. Is interpersonally exploitative, i.e., takes advantage of others to achieve his or her own ends.
7. Lacks empathy: is unwilling to recognize or identify with the feelings and needs of others.

8. Is often envious of others or believes that others are envious of him or her.

9. Shows arrogance, haughty behaviors or attitudes.[3]

Narcissism is a spectrum disorder, which means it ranges from a few narcissistic traits to full-blown narcissistic personality disorder (NPD). How common is narcissism? The American Psychiatric Association estimates that 2 to 16 percent of the people who are being treated by a mental health professional suffer from it, and it manifests in less than 1 percent of the general population.[4] In other words, the APA thinks it's rare. On the other hand, Jean Twenge and W. Keith Campbell, authors of *The Narcissism Epidemic: Living in the Age of Entitlement*, state, "Nearly 1 out of 10 Americans in their twenties, and 1 out of 16 of those of all ages, has experienced symptoms of NPD."[5] Twenge and Campbell believe that we are living in a narcissistic culture and that the incidence of narcissism is increasing.

I believe the truth lies somewhere between these two points of view. We all have some narcissistic traits and can occasionally behave in a narcissistic way. That does not mean we are narcissists. Given that narcissists generally do not seek treatment, I believe that narcissism is much more common than statistics would indicate. My research and clinical practice also support this view.

Let's spend some time getting to know the nine traits of narcissism by looking at examples of how they present themselves in love relationships. Remember, this is a spectrum disorder. The more of these traits a narcissist has, the more heartbreak he or she creates for the people in relationships with them.

The narcissistic personality:

1. *Grandiose sense of self-importance without commensurate achievements.* Example: The partner whose attitude is "When I say 'Jump!' you say 'How high?' " Jackie was the breadwinner for her family, which included her husband, a stay-at-home dad, and two children. Jackie expected the

family to organize all their activities around her. She was a finance executive for a car dealership, but to hear her talk, she owned and ran the company. They would be bankrupt without her! Jackie reminded her family constantly how smart she was. She clearly felt that others were beneath her.

2. *Fantasies of unlimited success, power, brilliance, beauty, or ideal love.* Example: The partner who constantly obsesses about status symbols. When Paul and Vicky went on vacation, Paul would always call local real estate agents, pretending to be in the market for a new or vacation home. He would present himself as a wealthy investor and insist that he needed a real estate agent sophisticated and connected enough to screen properties for him, so that he would see only the best of the best. While his income was middle-class, he would say things like "We really need a property that has a private landing strip, or at least room to add one. I travel a ridiculous amount, and I prefer to fly my own plane when I can. It's just more convenient." Vicky felt embarrassed to be pulled into this kind of lie and ashamed to be deceiving the real estate agents.

3. *Belief that he or she is special.* Example: The partner who regardless of income has to have the *best* divorce attorney in town. When seeking professionals to help with a divorce, such as evaluators and therapists for the children, the partner can only hire experts with PhDs who have studied at prestigious universities. If the judge does not rule in the narcissist partner's favor, that partner decides the judge is stupid and probably won't follow the court's orders. I recently observed a woman yelling at a judge, "You are just ridiculous. I am going to get a new judge!" She seemed to think this was as easy as exchanging a pair of shoes and was surprised when security removed her from the courtroom.

4. *Requires excessive admiration.* Example: The partner who is so needy that he or she solicits admiration all the time. My

client Tasha said, "Whenever we were going anywhere special, my partner Julia would always be the last one dressed. The whole family would be gathered in the hall, impatient and ready to go. Then Julia would make her entrance, coming down the stairs, preening and turning. She was waiting for everyone to go 'Ooooooooooh' and 'Aaaaaaaaah' and 'Mama, you're so *gorgeous*.' The kids and I would go over-the-top admiring her. We knew we weren't leaving the house until she got the admiration she wanted."

5. *Has a sense of entitlement and expects automatic compliance of others.* Example: Marcy felt she was entitled to pay less and demand more from the law firm she had retained. She refused to talk with the paralegals, always demanding to speak with "the attorney I am paying so much money to." If her hysterical demands were not met instantly, Marcy would threaten to change attorneys. Her favorite saying to her friends and family was "I will demand attention and be heard immediately, and if you don't believe me, just watch." Marcy's lawyer dumped her right before the proceedings began.

6. *Is interpersonally exploitative and takes advantage of others.* Example: The father who uses his children for his own ends. After Jeff and Heather got divorced, Jeff treated his daughter like an accessory. He realized that "there is nothing that makes a single man more attractive to women than walking around looking like a devoted father to his three-year-old daughter." He insisted that she dress in clothes that made her look upper-class and took her out to late-night dinners at restaurants. Once, when she became ill while visiting with him, he checked into a hotel so that the hotel staff would have to clean up after her vomiting. Jeff felt that he should not have to do this.

7. *Lacks empathy.* Example: The person who views any situation through the lens of what it means to him or her. Peter came home and said to his wife, "You know how my secretary has

that bad breast-cancer gene? The one that means she has to take time off from work every four months to have screenings? Well, right now, when we are under so much stress in the office, she's finally been diagnosed with breast cancer. I can't believe this is happening to me. She was also rattling on today about how worried she is about her kids and how they will handle this . . . hinting she might need more time off work. My business cannot handle this right now!"

8. *Is often envious or believes others are envious of him or her.* Example: The partner who cannot enjoy her husband's success. Brian was a new partner at a law firm and had just won a complicated and hard-fought trial. The law firm arranged a party to celebrate this victory and to thank Brian for his successful work. Brian wanted his wife, Beth, to attend the party and celebrate with him. Beth pretended that she would go and "acted" excited, but right before they left for the party, she decided to stay home because "I have better things to do!" She told Brian as he was walking out the door, "I think you won that case because I was listening to your whining every night. You couldn't have done it without me. I really don't have the time in my schedule to do that for you." Brian's excitement and pride in his work was blown to bits as he slowly drove to the party alone.

9. *Shows arrogance.* Example: The partner who is not particularly engaged with his child's accomplishments but wants to take all the credit for them. Jake attended a parent-teacher conference with his ex-wife and eight-year-old son, Mick. Mick was doing well in math, and his teacher was showing his papers and test scores to his parents, clearly wanting little Mick to have the lovely experience of being praised by a teacher in front of his parents. Jake interrupted the teacher abruptly and announced, "I can see where he gets his brilliance! I was always a star in mathematics as well and

in fact won a trip to an academic festival when I was much younger than Mick. It is also why I am doing so well in my engineering career. Yup, this kid gets his smarts from his dad. Nice going, son."

These nine traits describe why narcissists cannot love. They place primary importance on "what you can do for me" and expend a lot of energy on appearances. In a relationship with a narcissist, you will eventually realize that this person does not see the real you. You are the person's object to be manipulated for his or her own goals and needs.

My client Todd struggled to keep his voice steady as he said, "It is just so hard for me to realize that my wife is not capable of love. Our whole relationship was a farce. How could I have not seen it? It hurts me so much for our children as well. She can really never be the mother they need. None of our emotional needs were met, and I am just now understanding this."

Suzie was exasperated as she revealed, "I found out rather quickly that my husband would exaggerate his stories to make them sound better. He was often obnoxious to others, particularly those in the service industry. There seemed to be something missing in him. There wasn't a soul of deepness to him. He would fake this charming cuteness. I guess I should have figured this out sooner, like on the day of our wedding, when he was showing his actor side. In the wedding ceremony, I was looking at him and his body was turned to face all the people out in the audience. I whispered to him that he was supposed to be looking at me. He thought he was on a damn stage."

Is It Narcissism or Something Else?

If you have looked at the traits and examples above and said, "That's my partner and that's my life," then your partner likely has narcissistic traits or maybe even full-blown narcissistic personality disorder. You will probably never get an official diagnosis because your partner likely won't seek treatment. Even if you are in therapy, your therapist will only be able to make a secondhand diagnosis based on your reports about how your partner behaves.

People who are sociopathic, psychopathic, or abusive are extreme examples of narcissists. Other people who are emotionally limited may not be narcissistic. Asperger's syndrome, for instance, may be confused with narcissism because people with Asperger's are not as sensitive as normal people to emotional cues, but they do not mean to hurt or manipulate others. Narcissists generally know when they are hurting someone else and don't care.

In a blog post titled "Just Listen—Don't Confuse a Narcissist with Asperger's Syndrome," Dr. Mark Gouldston told a story about a father, a successful entrepreneur, who came with his fourteen-year-old daughter to Mark's office. When the daughter became distressed, her father looked bewildered, then started to cry. "My little girl is in awful pain and I think I somehow caused it. But I love her and that's the last thing I would ever want to do."[6]

The father had Asperger-like features but was sincerely upset at his daughter's sadness. He empathized, something narcissists are not capable of doing. Also, he perceived that he was responsible for her distress, which upset him. He felt accountable, which narcissists do not feel.

We will hear more stories as we go, but let's take some time to look at *your* story. I'm going to ask some questions about you, your partner, your relationship, and your children. As you go through this list, put a check mark next to any question you answer yes. The more questions you check, the more likely it is that your partner falls somewhere on the narcissism spectrum—maybe even has a full-blown narcissistic personality disorder.

Is Your Partner a Narcissist?

1. When something goes wrong, does your partner blame everyone but himself or herself?

2. Does your partner refuse to be accountable for his or her bad behavior? (For example, "*You* made me so mad that I couldn't help . . .")
3. Does your partner believe he or she is always right?
4. Is your partner unable to tune in to your feelings or your children's feelings?
5. Does your partner seem more concerned about how your behavior or your children's behavior reflects on him or her than on understanding and accepting who you and the kids are as people?
6. Does your partner seem to be out of touch with his or her own feelings or seem to deny them?
7. Does your partner carry grudges against you and others?
8. Is it all about your partner and his/her money, time, parenting time, property, and wishes/demands?
9. Does your partner seem unwilling to listen to you and to hear your concerns?
10. Is your partner constantly telling you what to do?
11. Does your partner make you feel "not good enough"? Have your partner's constant put-downs caused you to internalize this message?
12. Does your partner never ask about you, your day, or your feelings, even in passing?
13. Does your partner need to go on and on about how great he or she is and how pathetic you are?
14. Does your partner lie?
15. Does your partner manipulate?
16. Does your partner tell different people different stories about the same event, spinning the story so that he or she looks good?
17. When your partner talks about his or her kids, is it about what the kids *do* rather than who they *are*?
18. Are the children uncomfortable with your partner, love your partner, but at the same time are reluctant to spend time with him or her?

19. Have you come to realize that the kids protect themselves by not sharing their feelings with your partner?
20. Does your partner mistrust everyone?
21. Are the kids always trying to gain your partner's love and approval?
22. Has your partner spent minimal time with the children?
23. Does your partner typically skip the children's events if he or she does not have an interest in that particular activity or does not value it?
24. Does your partner push the children to be involved in activities that your partner likes or values and discourage or forbid them from pursuing activities that your partner does not value?
25. Have others in your life said that something is different or strange about your partner?
26. Does your partner take advantage of other people?
27. Is your partner all about power and control, pursuing power at all costs?
28. Is your partner all about image and how things look to others?
29. Does your partner seem to have no value system, no fixed idea of right and wrong for his or her behavior?
30. After the divorce, does your partner still want to exploit you? Or has your partner never calmed down?
31. When you try to discuss your life issues with your partner, does he or she change the subject so that you end up talking about your partner's issues?
32. When you describe your feelings, does your partner try to top your feelings with his or her own stories?
33. Does your partner act jealous of you?
34. Does your partner lack empathy?
35. Does your partner only support things that reflect well on him or her?
36. Have you consistently felt a lack of emotional closeness with your partner?

37. Have you consistently questioned if your partner loves you?
38. Does your partner do considerate things for you only when others are around to witness that good behavior?
39. When something difficult happens in your life (for instance, an accident, illness, a divorce in your family or circle of friends), does your partner react with immediate concern about how it will affect him or her rather than with concern for you?
40. Is your partner overly conscious of what others think?
41. Do you feel used by your partner?
42. Do you feel responsible for your partner's ailments or sicknesses?
43. Do you feel that your partner does not accept you?
44. Is your partner critical and judgmental of you and others?
45. Do you feel that your partner does not know and value the real you and does not want to know the real you?
46. Does your partner act as if the world should revolve around him or her?
47. Does your partner appear phony to you?
48. Does your partner swing from grandiosity to a depressed mood?
49. Does your partner try to compete with you?
50. Does your partner always have to have things his or her way?

As these questions show, narcissists are good at training you to doubt yourself. You may have come to feel that you are not good enough, and all bad outcomes are your fault, and even been conned into believing that you deserve nothing better.

Jeff, a client who had been partnered with Larry for eighteen years, described walking down the street and noticing a stylish young man coming in his direction, a man with a good haircut in some well-tailored pants. Jeff admired the man's subtle and thoughtful style. Then he realized that he was looking at his own reflection in a downtown store window. Larry had made him feel so ugly—his sense of self was so distorted—that he did not recognize himself.

Going through the checklist on pages 11–14 may be a shocking reality check for you as you realize that you have been duped, manipulated, or taken advantage of by a narcissist. Maybe you read the lists of narcissistic qualities in this chapter with a sinking feeling. The lists make a narcissist's traits suddenly seem so obvious that it is easy to get upset and think that you brought this on yourself, that you should have known. You may be furious as you remember the red flags that you chose to ignore. But give yourself a break. You're a good person. You just got deceived by someone who is practiced at deception. You are better, you deserve better, and you will get better.

There Is a Better Way

Recently, I logged on to Amazon.com to buy some hanging file folders for my office. I was trying to decide between three different options and decided to look at the customer reviews. You'll understand why this review caught my eye:

> If you're getting divorced you need these [file folders]. These will help you organize your soul-crushing divorce into easy-to-find packets of misery when you have to go to court to battle your insane drug-addicted ex (again) over custody of your two traumatized children. Don't put your pain in a pile! Let these hanging file folders neatly catalog the narrative of how you undid the worst mistake you've ever made. Your lawyer will thank you.[7]

If your partner is a narcissist, your life may feel like a train wreck right now, but you can get through this stage of your life. You can emerge stronger on the other side, even though you may need those file folders! But, first, we have to stay in this difficult place a little bit longer to understand how you got to where you are. Why did the narcissist target you? Why did you fall for the con job?

CHAPTER TWO

This Is Not the Person I Married: The Dynamics of the Relationship

Singer-songwriter Taylor Swift introduces her song "White Horse" by describing what it's like to fall for a narcissist:

> When I was a little girl, I used to read fairy tales. In fairy tales you meet Prince Charming and he's everything you ever wanted. In fairy tales the bad guy is very easy to spot. The bad guy is always wearing a black cape so you always know who he is. Then you grow up and you realize that Prince Charming is not as easy to find as you thought. You realize the bad guy is not wearing a black cape and he's not easy to spot; he's really funny, and he makes you laugh, and he has perfect hair.[1]

In this chapter, I will tell the sad-but-true stories of how anyone can be duped or conned by a narcissist, and how it might have happened to you. As you read these stories, don't be disheartened. You will learn more about how narcissists operate and you will understand why you were seduced by one. The artful charm of a narcissist in the beginning of a relationship is difficult to resist. You may discover that your personal history made you especially vulnerable to being trapped in the narcissist's sticky web. Please refrain from beating yourself up. Keep your mind open so that you can learn more about yourself and how to free yourself from your current situation.

In therapy, Mary Beth told me about her relationship with her first husband, George, a musician who was six years younger than she. Fun and nurturing in the courting period, George acted kind and understanding as Mary Beth was recovering from a horrible car accident. She credited him with helping her heal from that trauma. He listened to her and appeared to tune in to her emotional pain. Mary Beth felt lucky to have found George, but soon after they married, it all changed.

She learned early on that, if they were doing things he enjoyed, he was happy, so Mary Beth learned to cater to him. But when their first child was born, George believed Mary Beth only cared about the baby. He became quick to anger, often punching holes in walls and breaking things. At first she was shocked. Then George began to spend less and less time with the family. After George lost his job, he started acting coldly to Mary Beth and their son, and he started having affairs.

"I so wanted this to work, so we tried counseling, but he didn't like what three different counselors said about him," Mary Beth said. "One night a fight got physical and he really hurt me. I ended up in the hospital. I decided divorce was the answer and soon. But when I filed, things got even worse."

George hacked into her e-mail and Facebook. He took pictures of Mary Beth through a webcam he'd placed in the house. He even got a private investigator to follow her. In the divorce proceedings, George manipulated her so effectively that she stopped fighting for any kind of financial settlement.

"That's what I thought I had to do in order to get primary custody of my son," Mary Beth said. "George still blames me for everything, and I cannot manage to hold him accountable. Visitation and parenting decisions are an ongoing nightmare. Our son, who is now only ten, is unfortunately seeing how the world has to revolve around his dad. Does this ever end?"

Steven told me a similar story about how lucky he felt when he first met his wife, Sherri. Gorgeous, sexy, fun, and smart, she seemed to have it together. Steven admits they did party a little hard in the beginning, but he thought it was just part of dating and did not worry about it. They went on fabulous trips, took a couple of cruises, traveled to some distant cities and toured Europe. They both made good money in decent careers so life was good, until they married. After they tied the knot, the rose-colored glasses darkened.

Sherri began drinking more and demanded that Steven give her more attention. Steven tried to deny the problems. How could his princess have changed like this? Then Sherri became pregnant. Steven was overjoyed as he proudly announced the pregnancy to anyone who would listen. Then he realized, "Sher was a wreck. She obsessed about getting fat. She was told not to drink while pregnant and she didn't, but she started acting like a 'dry drunk.' She expected me to understand because she was pregnant." Sherri relapsed into bulimia while pregnant, throwing up to lose weight. "It was the toughest nine months of my life, or at least that's what I thought at the time," Steven said.

When the baby girl was born, Sherri did not want to breast-feed as she felt it was not sexy. As she obsessed about losing her post-baby weight, she developed anorexia. Being a stay-at-home mother did not suit Sherri; she hated it and began to drink heavily. "The day I came home from work to find my toddler wandering around the house while her mother was passed out on the couch, I filed for divorce," Steven said. "How did I not see this coming? It's taken me a long time to realize that this was not really a marriage. I'm not sure Sher really knew how to love. She was like an empty vessel that needed to be filled constantly or she would find ways to rebel or punish."

The same bait and switch occurred when Nancy met Chad, an anesthesiologist. Her whole family seemed charmed by him at first. Extroverted and talkative with a great sense of humor, he would come to dinner and put on a great show of being a smart doctor who could talk with anybody about anything. Nancy had become pregnant with her son when she was young but had not married the father and had

had a tough time as a single parent, living just above the poverty line. She was excited to be marrying someone with a good career and looked forward to moving up.

Before she married Chad, though, Nancy had a gut feeling that the relationship was not as good as it seemed. She noticed that Chad talked mostly about himself and his accomplishments. She was particularly concerned that he did not have a meaningful connection with his eleven-year-old son from a prior relationship. Interestingly, Nancy's father also had sensed something. On her wedding day, right before she and her father were to begin the procession down the aisle, Nancy mentioned some reservations she had about Chad. "I really thought my father would just say I was having wedding jitters or something like that, but he stopped in his tracks and said to me, 'Nance, if you want to call this off, I will go in there and explain to everyone that you are not marrying that man. You can take my car and leave right now and not have to face anyone. You just give me the go-ahead and I will do that for you.'"

Nancy did not call it off, but later wished she had. Chad turned out to be a narcissist who had no regard for others. In any situation, no matter what Nancy did, she was wrong and he was right. Nancy could have no life of her own as he controlled every aspect of it. He attempted to control her throughout the divorce proceedings and afterward. To this day, she asks herself, "Why did I not listen to my intuition?" Her greatest regret was having two children with Chad, because their father does not know how to love them. She loves her children, but feels bad for them almost daily as they are constantly hurt and pulled in different directions by him.

Who Is Most Vulnerable to Marrying a Narcissist?

We can all be vulnerable to con artists, and narcissists are skilled actors. They're good at presenting a tightly orchestrated image of what they want you to see and believe. They have an amazing ability to show the world only their chosen persona.

Based on my research and what I see in my practice, several factors make you more vulnerable to the narcissist's pursuit. The primary risk factor is having been raised in a family where one or both of your parents were narcissists. Children raised in narcissistic families have no role model for a healthy love relationship. They learn that love is about either "what I can do for you" or "what you can do for me." That sets them up for dependent or codependent relationships. As a result, adult children of narcissistic parents grow up with crippling self-doubt and a feeling of not being good enough. The overwhelming attraction you feel for a narcissist may be rooted deep in your unconscious, in a desire to master the trauma you experienced in being raised by a narcissist. Subconsciously trying to overcome your longing for acceptance and love and your lack of nurturance from the past, you may seek out a partner who is similar to your narcissistic parent.

"If my own mother or father could not love me, who will?" can be translated into "I am going to make sure this person loves me." You then find yourself trying to love enough, be enough, and do enough to *make* your partner love you: "If I couldn't do it in childhood, I will do it here." It's exhausting!

If you have not been in therapy to help you recover from an unloving parent, you may not understand these dynamics, which leaves you vulnerable to being sucked into a relationship with a narcissist. You may not feel that you deserved better, but you do.

In my first book, *Will I Ever Be Good Enough?: Healing the Daughters of Narcissistic Mothers*, I discuss what I call the Ten Stingers of relationship dynamics if you grew up with a narcissistic parent. Let's review those here.

The Ten Stingers: Relationship Dynamics of Being Raised by a Narcissistic Parent

1. You found yourself constantly attempting to win your parent's love, attention, and approval, but were never able to please.

2. Your parent emphasized the importance of "how it looks" rather than how it feels to you.

3. Your parent showed jealous tendencies toward you.

4. Your parent did not support your healthy expression of self, especially when it conflicted with his or her needs or was threatening in some way.

5. In your family, it was always about the narcissistic parent.

6. Your parent was unable to empathize.

7. Your parent could not deal with his or her feelings.

8. Your parent was critical and judgmental.

9. A healthy parental hierarchy was lacking and you were often treated more like a friend or a peer than a child.

10. Your family did not have healthy boundaries and you had little personal space or privacy.[2]

Raised amid these dynamics, you grow up feeling unimportant and not lovable. Your feelings were not validated. You learned to doubt yourself. Can you see how this would set you up to fall into the arms of the familiar narcissist and why you may not have trusted your red flags?

While having a narcissist for a parent is the biggest risk factor for being sucked into a familiar love relationship, it is not the only one. Other factors that make you vulnerable include past failed relationships, loneliness, lack of self-esteem, body-image issues, and starting to date too early after your last relationship ended. When you seek status from being in relationships, or value materialism over love, mutual respect, and emotional honesty, you also set yourself up for falling for a narcissist.

My client Jessica described her realization about her vulnerabilities: "I think I was vulnerable to finding a narcissist, but I think it was primarily fear based. I had never been married, and we are socialized to get married. I was getting older and I wanted to get married and start a family. I also think I wanted someone to take care of me."

This discussion about potential vulnerabilities to falling in love with a narcissist may be painful, but it's important to recognize how you were drawn into this relationship so that you won't repeat the pattern. Equally important for not repeating the pattern is a lesson on what a healthy relationship looks like.

Healthy Relationships

If you are in a bad relationship and that is your "normal" relationship, you may not have the life experience to know what a healthy relationship looks and feels like. This is especially true if you come from a dysfunctional family. Our narcissistic culture, which is all about image, can blind you to the qualities that matter in a life partner. For these reasons, it is important to discuss healthy relationships here.

So to begin, we have to throw out the old criteria of how we choose partners: "Is this person gorgeous?" "Does this person have health, wealth, and a great career?" "Is this person sexy?" "Does this person drive a cool, impressive, or classy car and wear great clothes?" Let's look at a new checklist:

The Healthy Relationship Checklist

1. Is this person kind and compassionate? Does he or she act with integrity? Is he or she good-looking on the inside?
2. Is this person committed to you? Does he or she have the capacity for a lifetime of learning and growing with you?
3. Is this person capable of genuine empathy? Is he or she willing to work through pain and problems?
4. Does this person have individual interests, hobbies, and passions, separate from yours?
5. Are most of your values and worldviews (philosophies of life) similar?
6. Do you share common interests so that you can be playful and spend leisure time together that you both enjoy?

7. Does this person have a sense of humor? Does he or she use it without hostility but with a good heart?

8. Does this person want to be your best friend and soul mate?

9. Does this person seem to be in touch with his or her own feelings and yours?

10. Can this person handle ambivalence and shades of gray and not be too rigid about failures and weaknesses in you, himself/herself, and others?

11. Does this person add to your soul life as well as your material life, thereby making your world a wonderful place to be when you are in it together?

12. Does this person bring out the best in you?

13. Is this person authentic?

14. Is this person capable of loving you and themselves in a healthy way?

15. Do you feel good about you in the presence of this person?[3]

Whether you are in a good or a bad relationship, the evolution of the relationship can be divided into three developmental stages. How you handle the challenges presented at each of these stages determines if you have a love that will last or if you will likely face turmoil and conflict.

The Stages of Relationships

Let's take a look at the three stages of how relationships develop. By understanding how a healthy relationship builds, we can contrast where and how things can go wrong.

STAGE ONE: LA-LA LAND

The most commonly understood stage of relationships is the first one, the romantic whirlwind of falling in love. I call this stage La-La Land because our senses are flooded. We are on cloud nine; everything is dreamy. We connect quickly and deeply with the other person and feel alive and excited. Passionate and exuberant about the many discoveries about your new love, you feel energy and joy. You're so happy, you're not even hungry. If you are older, being in La-La Land feels like being a teenager again as you rediscover the experience of lust and arousal. You are giddy that another person not only knows you, but also loves you and wants to live with you. You are not solitary in the world. You are known!

A client recently described it well: "I was so falling in love with this guy; it was a dreamy time. One day, I was just walking down the street and a truck driver leaned out of his window and yelled to me, 'Hey, lady! What's the secret? Why are you so happy?' "

If fear arises in La-La Land, you usually ignore it, which means you discount your intuition and refuse to see red flags that are popping up. During this phase, if friends or family notice something amiss and bring it to your attention, you are likely to dismiss their warnings. You are apt to give away your control and acquiesce to your partner to avoid conflict. If you get angry, you may try to suppress it for fear of falling off the floating cloud. Although this period is highly sexual and makes you feel vulnerable and important, you don't gain true emotional intimacy. Bruce Fisher, author of *Rebuilding: When Your Relationship Ends*, called this stage of love "blind and deaf." Is it any wonder we can make wrong love choices?

STAGE TWO: REALITY AND CONFLICT

La-La Land is lovely, but it doesn't last. When the giddiness ends, you fall back into the land of reality. This is when you start to become aware of the differences and tensions between you and your partner that are not trivial. Conflict begins, which is why this stage is called reality and conflict.

The Reality/Conflict Stage is normal and happens in every relationship. In this significant phase, people make one of three life-altering decisions:

1. There are conflicts that cannot be resolved. We do not have the interest or the motivation to do it, and we decide to leave the relationship.
2. We realize that we have a conflict, but we love each other. We decide to work through the conflict together, whatever needs to be done. If we need help, we go to therapy. Those in dedicated relationships stay together and work and play in sync because both parties are committed to learning, growing, and healing with each other.
3. We realize the conflict, find that we are not working through things, but we stay together anyway and are unhappy. Little resolution occurs in decision three, and the themes of our fights will surface often.

Unfortunately, far too many couples choose Door Number Three, which is why there are so many unhappy married couples today.

The biggest thing to look for in Reality/Conflict Stage is how you and your partner work together to solve your problems. Falling off the cloud, moving into reality, and "nesting together" all tend to bring out unresolved issues from your family of origin or prior relationships. This is the "baggage" that people drag with them into each relationship that needs to get sorted out together. How the couple resolves the issues that arise in this stage is important.

Do you communicate well? Does your partner want to learn and grow with you? Does it feel as if both of you get an equal say in resolving conflicts? This is a good time to assess your partner's capacity for empathy. Does your partner make a real effort to understand your point of view, even if it is different from his or her own?

This is also the time to pay attention to any red flags that come up, especially if you ignored them when you were in La-La Land. If you are in this stage, take a look at the narcissism checklist to see if you are dealing with a narcissist or someone with a lot of those traits. If he or she has narcissistic qualities, please take a step back and think about what you are doing and where you are going before you make a commitment to that person.

As a client who has done much recovery work described an ex-boyfriend, "When I met him, we seemed so compatible. We had similar interests, intellect, and value systems. We talked like crazy for hours. But one thing that began to bother me was that whenever I asked him how he was, he was always 'wonderful and fabulous,' and it couldn't be a better day! This was even true after he had minor surgery and I knew he was in pain. I began to wonder if he was in touch with his feelings at all. He seemed to need to present a positive image no matter what. I felt like I was not dealing with the *real* person here."

For narcissists, image is more real to them than reality. They lack a solid sense of self and cover that up by projecting a certain image no matter what is actually happening in their lives. When my client quickly broke up with this guy, although he had been telling her he was madly in love with her, he said he had been thinking about breaking up, too.

Another client realized she had been in denial for years. She told about being on a long taxi ride home with her then husband in NYC. Her ex was verbally abusive to her from the moment they entered the cab. He was dressing her down for everything, starting with a detailed assessment of her appearance. When they arrived at their apartment, her ex went right on in while she waited for the taxi driver to get the suitcases out of the trunk. As she paid him, he thanked her and added, "Hang in there, sister." "That got my attention. This total stranger could see what was going on in my life more clearly than I could."

Sometimes people do behave badly, even good people. You can give grace, and forgiveness, but the key is whether you work through conflicts with empathy for each other. If the relationship feels unhealthy and unresolvable, it's better for you to end it sooner rather than later. Sometimes you have great early chemistry with someone who turns out to be a bad match. If that's the case, you're probably also a bad match for that person.

STAGE THREE: EXPANDING

It's a shame that couples who are unable to resolve their conflicts in a healthy way can spend a lifetime in stage two. But couples who are able to work through their issues move into stage three, which I call Expanding.

The Expanding Stage is the real love experience. It means moving on in the relationship with a solid appreciation of each other and a healthy self-regard. You are loving, kind, and compatible and you validate each other's feelings. This love keeps growing and expanding into greater depths. You each own your individual issues. There is accountability, empathy, and good communication. You have learned to manage conflict. You expand individually and as a couple, growing in both self-understanding and emotional intimacy with your partner. Together, you create a secure, trusting, and rewarding environment. Vulnerability is the only route to intimacy. You now feel safe to allow this level of vulnerability. You see this both in your sexual relationship and in communication. And you're good with it.

Recently, a client gave me a passage written by the poet Rainer Maria Rilke in 1904. This is a beautiful explanation of expanding love:

> For one human being to love another human being: that is perhaps the most difficult task that has been entrusted to us, the ultimate task, the final test and proof, the work for which all other work is merely preparation. . . . Loving does not at first mean merging, surrendering, and uniting with another person (for what would a union be of two people who are unclarified, unfinished, and still incoherent?); it is a high inducement for the individual to ripen, to become something in himself . . . to become a world in himself for the sake of another person.[4]

If you are in a relationship with a narcissist, you will never get to this stage of love.

Putting It Together

Now that you have some assessment tools for evaluating your relationship, step back and think about what you have learned. Maybe your relationship problems are normal Reality/Conflict issues that you and your partner are going to resolve. That's great! Work it through. Get counseling if you need it. But if that's not the case, you are probably struggling with some uncomfortable feelings as you begin to realize that your chosen partner is a narcissist. You may feel intense shame and ask yourself, "Why did I make this horrible decision?" "What does this say about me?" "How did I get duped so badly?" "Is my relationship picker that messed up?" And the one I hear most often: "What have I done to my children?"

Please don't beat yourself up. But do consider these questions and answer them truthfully so it won't happen to you again. As my client Martha said, looking at the floor as she spoke, "This is so hard to discuss. How could I be so stupid? Of course nobody could be that awesome and love me that much every second. He put on quite the show. To this day, people say to me, 'What were you thinking?' But even my own family didn't see it. I felt not only shame, but also anger and frustration, and I blame myself. I got us all into this and why can't I fix it? It's just a terrible feeling. We have been divorced for years now and I still feel this way!"

Shame arises out of a feeling of failure. When you realize your relationship has failed, it is normal to feel shame. Many people in this difficult situation say they want to run, hide, or somehow become disconnected. Shame is dangerous because it takes over your whole being. Don't globalize your feeling of shame to include everything you do: "I have made a mistake, so I am a mistake."

Shame can deplete you. As my client Tom recounted, "I do seem to choose needy women, so I guess that's one clue to work on in therapy. Overall, the feeling of failure is overwhelming."

Shame needs to be released and healed or it can cause other problems, such as depression, addiction, eating disorders, and even aggression. We will come back to this later in the book when I talk about recovery. Empathy and compassion for yourself will cure this.

Now that we have explored the territory of narcissism and, I hope, given you a better idea of why you have ended up with a narcissistic partner, the question "Should I stay or leave?" looms.

If you need more time to digest the first two chapters, give yourself that opportunity before we move to decision-making.

PART TWO

BREAKING FREE

CHAPTER THREE

I'm Married to a Narcissist: Stay or Leave?

If your marriage or relationship is dysfunctional, should you stay or leave? This one question triggers many other questions, especially if you have been in a long-term relationship. You may have a home, a career, a community, joint finances, and in-laws to figure into your decision-making. If you have children, the decision is even more difficult. You want to do what is best for your children, but this chapter focuses only on you, the adult. We will consider decisions about your children later.

Denial

At this point you may ask yourself, do I really have to make a decision? You may feel you can postpone leaving. As Jim Butcher, author of the fantasy novel *Turn Coat*, states, "The human mind isn't a terribly logical or consistent place. Most people, given the choice to face a hideous or terrifying truth or to conveniently avoid it, choose the convenience and peace of normality. That doesn't make them strong or weak people, or good or bad people. It just makes them people."[1]

Many of us facing difficult decisions avoid making them. You are using this book to educate yourself to make the best decision for you and your family. No one else can tell you what to do. This is your life. You are the person who will live with the decisions that you make.

Even after you understand the common dynamics of being in a narcissistic relationship, you may wish and hope that things will change. This is a natural desire. No one wants to pull the rug out from under his or her entire life. We change things only when we are ready.

I encourage you to make a list titled "To Stay or to Leave." This list should reflect your value system and should include basic but important considerations such as personal safety and mental health, physical health, finances, support systems, and the safety and mental and physical health of your children. Because this list has to reflect your life and value system, it is not appropriate for me to give you one to follow. If you are stumped as to where to begin, please refer back to the questions in the list "Is Your Partner a Narcissist?" and answer them with your safety, health, and support systems in mind.

Denial can be tough to break through. As Cara told me, even though she knew something was a little off before she and her husband married, she just kept thinking he would change. "He had these temper tantrums when things did not go his way, and the episodes got closer and closer together. Then he would kind of come around and act nice, but his verbal abuse was difficult to get over. He would blow up and then act like nothing happened. I would hang on to the good times, hoping they would last, but it was almost like a cycle or pattern for him."

Even as they were being married, she had reservations. She cried so much on their wedding day that even he noticed and asked why.

"I think I knew then that it was not right, that I was making a huge mistake," Cara said. "When I look back, I can see the major denial and can hardly believe it now. I wanted to believe he really loved me."

Lucy remembered her ex's rage attacks. "I remember one time we were checking out of a hotel. We were running late for our flight, which was totally his fault, by the way, and he was screaming at the bellhop. The bellhop and I were managing all the luggage, and there was a lot of it. My ex was not carrying anything. He was just making demands on us and criticizing every single thing we did. I said under my breath, 'Oh my God, he's an asshole.' The bellhop heard me and said, 'Yes, I know!' We made the flight, and then all of a sudden my ex was all sweetness and light. He said, 'You look tired. Do you want a pillow? Can I get you a blanket?' I always waited for his nice side to show up, hoping and wishing things would be different."

We can all get stuck in denial. When we marry or enter a relationship that we want to work but find it's dysfunctional, we ask ourselves what we can do to make it better, instead of confronting the reality that we can't fix it on our own. When we start to realize that nothing we do seems to help, many people decide they need to get therapy to understand themselves and their relationship better.

Couples Therapy

If you are unsure whether your marriage can be healed, and if your partner is willing to try, couples therapy is a good idea. It is important to understand how couples therapy should work, however. Let's look first at how couples therapy works without narcissism, so you have a benchmark for comparing your situation.

After being in a relationship for a time, we tend to develop some negative behaviors that can almost take on a life of their own. Our interactions repeat and repeat almost independent of what created the conflict. In normal couples therapy, partners who have developed negative habits try to break out of their toxic two-step by finding better ways to communicate their feelings. An argument about some minor household chore, such as emptying the dishwasher, for instance, regularly escalates into reviving old disputes. Good couples therapy will help you figure out what triggers your cycle of miscommunication and teach you new ways of interacting that will replace the old.

In couples work, the partners explore the recurring themes in their relationship. Most people think they are fighting about specific topics, such as parenting, money, sex, or who does more housework. When they explore these conflicts, deeper issues and emotional dynamics come to light. Each recurring argument needs to be examined to uncover buried emotions, which are usually "I don't feel loved," "I don't feel respected," "I don't feel heard," and "I don't feel appreci-ated." The couple's disputes typically contain more depth and pain than they realize.

I teach couples to recognize the difference between context and feelings. I draw a big box on a piece of paper and another smaller box directly below it. In the top box, we write the common theme or con-text of the argument that we have discovered. In the second box, we write the feelings associated with the argument. Teaching couples to leave the top box alone and focus on the bottom box helps them to tune in to each other more empathetically and care for each other's perspectives. When they do this, both partners feel heard and vali-dated. All of a sudden, they find it much easier to solve the top-box argument.

Because we all bring our past into our relationships, couples ther-apy helps us understand how our history affects the way we interact with our partner. It is especially helpful for partners to recognize each other's triggers even in the midst of a battle so they can decide if this is their issue or their partner's. Knowing that can help you be more accountable.

Some partners need to have individual therapy for a time before couples therapy can work. If you are with a partner who is capable of this kind of in-depth work, however, it is not likely that you are in-volved with a narcissist.

Couples Therapy When One Party Is a Narcissist

If you are in a relationship with a narcissist, couples therapy is usually not effective. You may not even be able to get your partner to partic-ipate. Narcissists do not see themselves as the problem. They might come for one couples session in order to tell the therapist how awful you are and to describe your specific problems, but they never admit to faults of their own. Usually, they will find reasons to avoid therapy. They'll construct arguments to show why it is a bad idea. If they do attend, they often blame the therapist for creating the problem or declare that the therapist is "not good enough"—not educated enough or smart or skilled enough to understand them and their importance and viewpoints. They may become agitated and yell at you and the therapist and walk out of the session.

Maggie described attempting couples work with her spouse before she realized he was a narcissist. She wasn't feeling strong before they entered the therapist's office as she was suffering from low self-esteem, weight issues, and clinical depression. "I had been prescribed an antidepressant and was trying that when we started our couples work. But even getting to the first session was hard. He did not believe in therapy. He started in, taking control, and to my surprise was spouting off about how fat I was, and how I was this mess of a depressed woman who needed drugs. Everything was my fault and I was the one who needed therapy and then all would be well. When the therapist suggested that staying in the marriage might not be the best thing, he got up and walked out! That was it. He would never go back. Throughout the entire divorce and all the court battles, he clung to his view that it was all my fault. I was depressed and overweight!"

Andrew remembered his similar marriage-counseling experience. At the first session, his ex-wife immediately started describing how Andrew was the problem. "She rationalized all her bad behavior, including her infidelity. I heard everything that she felt I did wrong. She made it sound like I was some bad dude. All I tried to do was take care of her and the children. It was not like I was living some big fun life. But the marriage counselor told me, 'I don't think she knows how to be in a relationship or how to love. I don't think the river runs that deep within her. She has a soft spot for you, but she does not know who you are.' The marriage therapist felt she just wanted a glamorous life and a daddy."

As a therapist, when I am dealing with a narcissist, I can feel something is missing right away. A narcissist does not go to counseling to get help, but rather to manipulate the situation to try to get his or her way. Narcissists often have a combative attitude and question and disagree with everything I say. When the partner tries to speak, the narcissist interrupts and tries to take control. Sometimes, such people even ask me inappropriate personal questions, trying to "get" me on something. When I ask narcissists to listen to their partner, they put on this *How dare you?* look. One narcissist actually got out $100 bills and a cigarette lighter and started to set the bills on fire, saying, "This is what I think of your therapy, Doctor!"

In couples therapy, when you or your therapist use the term *empathy*, the narcissist will have no idea what you are talking about. Narcissists typically say, "Am I missing something here?" Well, yes, they are! One client with narcissistic traits actually said to me, "How is my lack of empathy my problem?"

Sometimes, narcissists may say the correct words and apologize for causing their partner pain. They may even mimic the therapeutic language they've been told they should use. But they do not follow through with heartfelt care in their actions. You may feel hopeful about therapy at first with narcissists who are playing along, but you learn they are only playing a game to manipulate you, and they will go back to being "all about themselves." If you feel that the therapist is being influenced by the charm or presentation of the narcissist, you should talk individually with the therapist to express your concerns. If that is not successful, don't invest more energy with someone who does not get it—you need to change your therapist.

Can a Narcissist Truly Love?

From my clinical and personal experience, I think that full-blown narcissists cannot truly love. Love is tuning in to another person emotionally, and narcissists are incapable of that. If you are in a relationship with a narcissist, you have probably rarely felt loved or accepted, except in the early stages. You get constant messages of "You are not good enough." You are told daily about all the things you do wrong and need to change. You are not heard, seen, or validated. Your feelings are usually ignored or dismissed. You are expected to perform and be who your partner wants you to be rather than being loved for who you are. That you have not felt loved in this relationship is a difficult thing to accept.

Bob described how his wife, Melissa, handled his grief at the sudden death of his mother. "A few months after we married, I got a call that my mother was being taken to the hospital for some emergency surgery. We were preparing to go when I got a second call that she died suddenly before they got her into surgery. This threw me into deep despair and grief. Not only did my new wife, Melissa, not want to attend the funeral with me, but in the months to come while I was grieving and in shock, she would say to me, 'Go talk to your friends about this, I am tired of hearing about your feelings. If had known you were this emotional, I would not have married you. There is something wrong with you. You need to pull it together fast.' Then she walked over to me and kicked me in the shins and spat on me! I cannot tell you the shock. To this day, I think of this incident and wonder how I stayed in that relationship so long, trying and trying to make it work. I beat myself up for years, thinking I was just a wimpy man. I understood much later that I was simply grieving and this was completely normal."

Liza talked about how her partner, Mary, was so attentive in the beginning of the relationship that Liza felt truly loved. Then things changed. "We decided to have a child together using artificial insemination, with me carrying the baby. I was very thin when we met, but getting pregnant, I did gain weight and had trouble postpregnancy losing the extra pounds. Suddenly, I was being criticized and judged constantly about the weight. One day she even said to me, 'You are disgustingly obese now and unattractive. No one would want to have sex with you or even touch you.' She stopped our intimate relationship then and there. I was too fat! I no longer was the image of what she wanted in a partner, I guess. And now, we had this precious child, too!"

Betty told that when her ex was angry with her, he would wait until she was asleep and then push her out of the bed and onto the floor. Tricia had similar difficulties sleeping in the same bed with her husband: "If I had to get up in the night to use the bathroom and I woke my ex, he would be so angry that, when I returned to bed, he would kick me viciously." Not nice bedtime stories!

Love to a narcissistic partner is like having a shiny new bike to ride. Narcissists like the look of a new bike and the sight of themselves with one, but they don't actually know how to ride. They do not have the skills to make the wheels go round or the balance to stay seated and moving. Underneath their grandiosity, focus on appearances, and need for constant praise and attention, they are unhappy people.

The Debilitating Effects of Narcissism on Families

Narcissists want to control everything about you, and they will want to control your children, too. The narcissist does not feel secure enough to allow each individual in the family to have his or her own sense of self, beliefs, decisions, and separate interests. They expect all family members' lives to revolve around them, and they ignore other people's needs or desires. There is no sense of community or individuality. Their needs rule.

Family life with a narcissist can be frightening, said Jeff, who was married to Meg for eleven years. "She was a tyrant. She had to rule the roost. If I tried to assert myself, she put me in my place. I tried to keep peace between everybody. Our son was terrified of her. His little legs would just shake. It was then that I decided I needed to get out. She never forgives anything, whether you did it or not. She was angry ninety percent of the time. She had relationship problems with everyone . . . her family, the neighbors, and at work. But it was always someone else's fault, not hers. I worry terribly about my two kids!"

Sarah remembers the constant tension of life with her ex-husband, David. "He was obsessive about cleanliness. He expected dinner on the table at five p.m. sharp, the house perfectly clean at all times, and complete order in the household. Our daughter loved helping in the kitchen and set the table as soon as she was old enough. I would put out the plates, silverware, and glasses to let her arrange it all. She started this at about age five. As soon as Dave saw this, he started in with her about the perfect way to set the table. The knife goes here and the spoon goes there. If she did it wrong, he would turn everything upside down on the table. To this day, and she is a teen now, she won't set the table when her father is around. This guy had to rule everything. I had to carefully pick the battles so our child was not constantly seeing the conflict."

Barbara remembered waking up in bed one morning dizzy and disoriented. "I was panicked, it was clearly an emergency. Fortunately my cousin was visiting. We were about to rush out to the doctor when my husband entered the kitchen and said, 'Can you be sure to make my bed before you leave?' My cousin gasped, and all I could think was thank goodness she was there as I needed someone to drive me to the doctor."

Joseph tells another short, revealing anecdote. "My ex asked me for a plate. I got a plate and put it in front of her and she said, 'Oh, that's not where I wanted it.' She looks for people and situations she can pounce on when she's in a bad mood."

Healthy relationships require reciprocity, communication, and sharing of decision-making. Narcissists use their power and control to get their way. They are not able to see what they do to you or the children. We will talk about that soon, but let's continue to explore why you are staying or stayed in the relationship.

What Keeps You There?

Maybe you believe in your gut that leaving would be the right thing for you to do, but you just can't do it. If that's your story, it's time to think about the barriers or blocks that are keeping you there. You might also consider having some individual therapy to help you reflect.

One client told me she couldn't leave until the children were grown. She plans to leave *later*. In the meantime, she has what I call a "civil connect" with her spouse. That means she tries hard not to have arguments or be vulnerable with him. She is using the time before she leaves to do her recovery work, so that when she does leave, she is prepared. This same woman recently went to the doctor because she was not feeling well and was told that her blood pressure was so elevated that she was at risk for a stroke. She works out regularly and eats a balanced diet. The doctor said it was her stress. She is only thirty-three. With this kind of health problem, perhaps she would be better off making the break from the relationship sooner than later.

While emotional abuse is not life-threatening in the short term, it is life-destroying in the long term. It is important to assess what being in this relationship is doing to the real you. How is it harming you? What are the effects on your well-being? Do you feel you have lost your sense of self? Is the trauma of this relationship catching up to you?

Only after Tonya divorced her husband did she realize that she had totally lost herself in the relationship. "My self-esteem and sense of worth were demolished! I was constantly told how stupid I was and how incompetent in everything I did. I was not a good mother, good wife, good housekeeper, good anything! I was in a severe depression. I felt like a blank sheet of paper. When I first met with my divorce attorney, it was a three-hour meeting, and the whole time I was so shamed and felt so low that I could not look at him. If I started to cry, I would apologize. To this day, after three years of being out of this horrible marriage, I am still trying to rebound. I still don't even make eye contact with a man in the grocery store."

Michael went to a therapist to get beyond agonizing about his decision to leave his partner. The final words he heard loud and clear from his therapist were "Michael, you can stay right where you are and make no changes for your life, and I predict that you will become a psychiatric number."

Judy had a hard time getting the energy to leave because living with someone she had to constantly manage exhausted her. "I was daily setting boundaries with him. It was not a partnership or union, it was his show. No matter what the subject was, he was the one doing all the talking. There came a time when I just stopped talking. I wasn't being heard anyway. I was losing me."

Feeling worse than exhausted, Jack was passively suicidal in his relationship. "I began to realize if I stayed with her, I was going to die. Not that she would kill me, but that I would end up with some kind of anxiety disorder, die of some stress disease or heart attack. That's how stressful it was. I am a recovering alcoholic, and I could have gone back to drinking. It really began to scare me for my own well-being. I realized I was doing unsafe things like not wearing my seat belt and driving faster than I should at times. I think my spirit was dying."

Religious Barriers

Maybe your religious views are keeping you in your marriage. If so, you may want to seek counsel from your church or pastor. While some religious groups never accept divorce, most are open to discussions about divorce if it is best for you and your children, especially if there is physical and emotional abuse. Nonetheless, religious counselors have their own strengths and weaknesses, knowledge and blind spots, just like the rest of us. I have heard both good and bad stories from people who sought pastoral counsel.

Marion and her husband, Ted, were Roman Catholics and quite religious, but Marion desperately wanted out of the relationship because Ted was horribly emotionally abusive. Ted insisted on talking to their priest in hopes he could talk her out of it, and, in fact, the priest reflexively sided with Ted and said, "We teach not to leave your spouses." Immediately after he said this, Ted got down on his knees and begged Marion to stay. Marion looked at the priest, who was crying and feeling bad for Ted, but kept her wits about her. She told the priest that Ted was abusive, and the priest asked Ted if that was so. Ted did not deny it, but he blamed it on Marion, saying that she just made him so upset. After this emotionally draining session, the priest went to Marion's father to discuss what was best for the couple.

Thankfully, Marion saw through the complicity of these men and freed herself from her abusive marriage.

By contrast, Cathy told this story: "The day after I left my husband, I met with a pastor who had been recommended by a friend. I revealed how guilty I felt about having ended the marriage and then told him about the abuse my husband had heaped on me day after day. The pastor looked at me and said, 'Everything that you have said tells me that your husband ended the marriage years ago by the way that he treated you. You did what you needed to do to protect yourself and your daughter. I hope that you can learn to let go of that feeling of guilt.' "

As Cathy's story shows, not all religious counselors will tell you to remain in the marriage. Brian said he talked to his religious counselor days before filing for a divorce. He reported that his chaplain told him, "I am not in the marriage-breakup business, but it is time to move on. I think your wife is running from a hole in her heart and lives in deep shame."

Concerns about Money

When financial concerns are the major barrier to leaving a bad marriage, you should consult with a divorce attorney in advance of taking any legal action. A skilled attorney can examine your financial situation and give you an idea of what is likely to happen in a divorce. You must have a realistic understanding of what your finances are likely to be after divorce.

My client Fatima shared how hard it was for her to answer those who asked her why she stayed with her husband for as long as she did. "The honest truth is that money had a lot to do with it. I came from a working-class background. Every paycheck was spoken for five different ways. When I was married to Hank, we could pay all our bills and still put money in the bank. I just did not want to leave that. But when I finally understood what being married to him was doing to me, how it was destroying me, I got to the point where I said, 'I would have a better life if I moved back to my parents and worked at McDonald's.' "

Physically Abusive Relationships

You may be thinking, "My partner does not hit me, so maybe he or she is not narcissistic." All narcissists are psychologically and emotionally abusive. Some are physical or sexual abusers as well. Sociopaths and psychopaths are narcissistic at the core of their being.

A therapist's job is to assist you in making healthy decisions for yourself. We generally do not tell you what to do, but in cases of abuse, a different rule applies. We want to protect you from harm, and everyone needs to protect children from abusive and dangerous environments. If you are with an abuser, get out. Please do not take chances.

In many relationships, one partner wished and hoped that things would get better, but their lives ended tragically.

When Amy discovered that her husband was sexually abusing one of her children, she was shocked. She had had no idea of the abuse until her child reported it to an adult friend, and the friend reported it to authorities. Investigators determined that the child was telling the truth and arrested the husband. Amy's husband was the primary breadwinner, but she immediately began divorce proceedings and fought for custody of her three children. She would not put the children at risk one minute more.

Another client named Joe was a strong man who had been taught to handle problems the way a guy should. Be tough. Fix it. But when he discovered that his wife was physically abusing their young children, he, too, left and fought for custody. It was a tough battle because even though his wife was unstable, courts, even seeing a history of physical abuse, attempt to keep both parents in the children's lives.

If you or your children are experiencing physical or sexual abuse at the narcissist's hands, then you need to leave. Do not stay in a dangerous situation. There is no further assessment needed. Get away.

Take Care of Yourself!

If possible, keep a private journal about your relationship and record the emotional or verbal abuse. Take a serious look at the psychological harm that you have suffered in this relationship. It is real. Try to keep the focus in your journal on how your relationship has harmed you. This will help you see the prevalence, frequency, and patterns of the abuse. If you are tempted to forgive and try again, you can do so with the full knowledge and memory of prior problems, and you can assess whether your partner has changed in how he or she treats you. You only get this one life here on earth. You deserve love, peace, and a joyful existence. You do.

Judge your relationship and life for yourself. People outside your relationship—friends, family, coworkers, neighbors—have different kinds of dealings with your spouse. Some may have been taken in by the practiced charm. These people will think what they think—you can't control that. That's okay. They don't have to get it. But you do!

I often tell this story to my clients who are making a life-changing decision: Imagine that you are on a big log, out in the middle of a fast-moving river. It's a scary place to be. If you jump off one side, you will be swimming back to the familiar shore of what you know. If you jump off the other side, you will be swimming toward a place unknown to you. We are always afraid of the unknown. So you just stay a little while longer on the log . . . but you begin to get dizzy. So you jump off and begin swimming toward that new and unfamiliar territory, and you swim like hell to get there. Once you are there, you look back and say, "That was a good decision!" You are competent and capable of making a good decision. But while you're swimming furiously after you've made your decision, you don't always know or believe it was right.

One client received a Valentine's card from her narcissistic partner that was the turning point for her. The card said "Happy Valentine's Day" on the front, and inside the spouse wrote, "You need to love me more." Then he signed his full name in cursive, sprawled across the card. It was all about him. Clearly she needed a relationship in which she received more love. This card was her final signal to jump off the log and swim away from her self-involved partner.

If you are considering divorce from a narcissistic partner, I know you are worrying about the children in more ways than one. You are worrying for good reasons, which I will address in the next chapter.

CHAPTER FOUR

What Is Best for My Children?: Help with Divorce Decisions

Good parents who are considering divorce always struggle to answer "What is best for my children? Is it better for them if I stay in this marriage or would it be better for them if I divorce?"

The best situation for children is to live with two parents who love each other in a committed relationship. These parents each bring special gifts to their children, who benefit from their parents' different perspectives and styles.

Numerous studies have been made about the effect of divorce on children. The older studies from thirty years ago looked at children whose parents had gotten divorced and compared them to children whose parents had not. As a group, the children who came from "intact" families were happier than those whose parents had gotten divorced. But since people in good marriages usually don't get divorced, of course their kids would be happier and less stressed than children from the divorce group.

In the last ten years, more informative studies have looked at the effect of parental conflict on children in intact families and found it to be significantly damaging to children. Children who grow up in environments with perpetual conflict more often develop problems such as anxiety, sleep disorders, depression, eating disorders, and aggression. They are more vulnerable to suicidal tendencies and to unhealthy relationships. Children whose parents are mentally ill tend to develop chronic illnesses and emotional illnesses.

The question that you really want to ask is "Is it better for *my* children if I stay married or get divorced?" As you think about this question, it's important to understand that the choice that you have is not divorce versus a happy marriage. The choice you have is:

- Stay married to your narcissist spouse and raise your children in a home with all the stress that living with a narcissistic parent creates for you and your children every day, or
- Divorce your narcissist spouse. Your children will still have one narcissist parent, but the amount of stressful time your children spend with him or her may be limited.

As you wrestle with these two choices, you want to be sure you are asking yourself these questions: "What does it mean to a child to grow up in a home where one parent is a narcissist and where there is high conflict?" and "What are the specific issues and challenges that come up for children in divorce, and especially in a divorce where one parent is a narcissist?

Some things about your situation you truly cannot change. You cannot change that your partner, the father or mother of your children, is a narcissist. As much as you might want to, you are not going to be able to sever your partner's connection with your children. However, you can decide whether to stay or to go, and that decision—whichever way you make it—will affect your children's lives.

Reflect on the wisdom of the Serenity Prayer:

God grant me the serenity
To accept the things I cannot change;
Courage to change the things I can;
And wisdom to know the difference.[1]

You have it in your power to look at these difficult choices, to choose, and to commit yourself with courage to the choice that seems best for your own heart and for your children.

What If You Stay?

Let's say that you don't get divorced. You stay married to your narcissist spouse. What will that mean to your children?

In my first book, *Will I Ever Be Good Enough? Healing the Daughters of Narcissistic Mothers*, I focused on understanding the long-term, insidious harm suffered by girls who grow up with a narcissistic mother. I focused that book on mothers and daughters, but all children raised by a narcissistic parent suffer emotional harm. The dynamics may be different for boys and girls, and also different depending on whether the mother or the father is the narcissist, but narcissistic parents cause serious harm to all their children.

What kind of harm are we talking about? The effects are as individual as the parents and children are, but a child with a narcissistic parent is at minimum at risk for many of the problems suffered by those who grow up in a high-conflict household: low self-esteem, post-traumatic stress disorder, depression, anxiety, eating disorders, and other mental health problems. Such children are also at risk in their future adult relationships. They may become narcissistic themselves or they may be drawn to a narcissist.

Narcissistic parents are unable to love and empathize with any other human being, even their own children. In their book *The Narcissistic Family: Diagnosis and Treatment*, therapists Stephanie Donaldson-Pressman and Robert M. Pressman describe how children raised by a narcissistic parent do not get their emotional needs met. Instead of the parent's supporting and nurturing the child, the parent is only interested in his or her own needs, leaving the child to grow up feeling "defective, wrong, and to blame. When one is raised unable to trust in the stability, safety, and equity of one's world, one is raised to distrust one's own feelings, perceptions, and worth."[2]

One teenage girl I interviewed explained it like this: "With my mom, it was always conditional love. I would only be loved for the way she wanted me to be. If I didn't agree to her terms of what kind of daughter I should be, then it wouldn't be love. On many occasions she has told me she loves me, but her actions speak very differently. It was always very confusing as a kid. . . . I started having really bad anxiety, agoraphobia and panic attacks."

Take a moment to think about the love that you have for your children. It's different from the love that you have for another adult. The normal, healthy love of a parent for a child is pure and unconditional, immense and unbounded. People of faith compare it to God's love. You put your child's interests ahead of yours. But this is not what narcissistic parents do, as many of my patients have described.

In one interview, a mother expressed her sadness about her husband's behavior toward their two children. She said, "On the inside, he was very shallow. He never spent quality time with our daughter. . . . My son would like to have more time and attention [from his dad], but he never does dad type of stuff. It's not his priority so it's not going to happen. You wouldn't know it by listening to him talk or looking on his Facebook, but the kids will give you a completely different story. What he shows the world and what the kids know is totally different."

Years ago, Dr. Gordon Livingston, author of *How to Love*, gave his working definition of love: "The question is 'Would you take a bullet for this person?' "[3]

It is difficult for people who are unfamiliar with narcissism to understand the subtle and insidious emotional distortions that are routine in families with a narcissist parent. Even the innocent spouse and the children in these families can have a hard time explaining the emotional minefield they walk through every day. The other family members are expected to read the narcissist's mind, one client said, and meet every unspoken need. "It virtually assures that no one's needs will ever be met: I will not get what I want, and you will be a failure because you did not provide it. This is truly a lose-lose scenario. In families where mind reading is a requisite in interpersonal relations, the word *should* is used a lot ('he *should* have known that I needed him home; he *should* have noticed that I never wear blue')."[4]

A child raised in a family with those dynamics will have trouble growing up into an adult who is able to express his or her needs in a straightforward, nonmanipulative way.

A client named Priscilla told me about the incident that gave her the courage and strength to leave her husband. Priscilla's husband, Henry, had full-blown narcissistic personality disorder and was also physically abusive. They had one child, a little boy, who was three years old at the time of this incident.

"I had actually left my husband several times, but I always ended up going back," Priscilla said. "There were a lot of reasons. One day I was talking to my doctor about it, and he said, 'I want you to understand something. We know—because there has been a lot of research in this area—that when children grow up in a family where there is abuse, they are very likely to grow up and repeat that pattern in their own lives. When you stay in this marriage, you are making a decision for your three-year-old son that he will become either an abuser or an abused spouse. If you cannot find the strength to leave for yourself, then ask yourself if you can do it for your son.'

"Just one week after that conversation, I was at a restaurant with my husband and son, Stuart. Stuart got angry about something. He looked at me and said, 'If you don't do what I want, I am going to fucking kick you and kick you until you do.' My husband thought it was funny. He actually laughed. Then he said, 'Way to go, Stuart.' But it crystallized the decision for me. I took one week to plan, and then I left him for good. I did not want my wonderful son to grow up and be like his dad."

Not all narcissists are physically abusive, but this story clearly shows the negative effects on children of staying in a marriage with physical abuse.

How much harm your children will have growing up in an intact family with a narcissist depends on where your spouse is on the narcissism spectrum. How damaged are you? Can you balance some of the harm done by your spouse by being extra empathetic with your children? Can you do that within your marriage? You are the only person who can answer these questions.

What If You Leave?

To begin with the positive, when you divorce a narcissist, your children experience some real benefits:

1. You will be taking your child out of daily conflict.
2. You will have an immediate opportunity to create a healthier home environment.
3. You will have more time for your children because you won't have to give top priority to your needy narcissist spouse.
4. You will be taking your child out of a home environment dominated by a narcissist parent. Even if you are not happy with the custody arrangement, you will be giving your child a much greater opportunity to spend time with healthy people.
5. You will be able to show your child a healthy role model for relationships, starting with healthy parenting.
6. You will likely find that your children are relieved.

Unfortunately, divorce is going to be tough on you and tough on them, because divorcing a narcissist is not like a "normal" divorce.

What Does a "Normal" Divorce Look Like When You Have Children?

Let's first look at how divorce normally works when a couple have children. When I refer to "normal" divorce, I am talking about divorce involving two parents who are reasonably sane and in stable mental health but who decide that their marriage cannot or should not be saved. Maybe one partner wants to break up and the other doesn't. It may not initially be a mutual decision, but, in the end, both parties agree the relationship cannot be salvaged.

In a normal divorce, the parties get through the process without extreme or prolonged conflict. Sometimes, if they have a decent agreement about how the divorce should work, they don't involve attorneys or other professionals. They get divorce paperwork from the court and fill it out themselves. Sometimes a divorcing couple will hire one attorney to help them both with the legal matters. Or they may each get an attorney to assist with their specific rights to property, assets, debt, and decisions about the children. If there is a disagreement about custody or visitation, they may choose to have professional evaluations done, but usually they work out plans that they both agree will work for the children. Many times a mediator helps them iron out the details, and many skilled divorce mediators are available.

In many divorces in this country, loving parents have worked out creative, thoughtful ways to do what is in the best interests of their children. Such parents usually communicate well and focus on what is best for the kids. They may have parenting plans on paper, but they are flexible when they need to be and can adapt the plan without going back to court. These couples have made decisions to be apart, but are sincere and earnest about continuing to coparent after the divorce.

Some parents decide to live close to each other. They work together to coparent the kids even after divorce. In other situations, one party moves out of state and the children spend the school year with one parent and summers with the other, sharing holidays in ways that work for the children's schedules.

With these kinds of "normal" divorces, the adults are eventually fine with both attending events that involve the children. They introduce each other to their new partners and encourage the children to have healthy relationships with both their stepparents and birth parents. For events such as weddings, births, graduations, and funerals the adults and children attend and participate together. Such divorced couples manage their emotions and make reasonable decisions about both divorce and custody.

Jenna and Jim had a normal divorce motivated in part by Jim's having had a previous marriage end in an extremely contentious and expensive divorce that had damaged his daughter from that marriage. He did not want to repeat history. Jenna was sad that their marriage had failed, but she was not vindictive. She did not need to "win," and she did not want to make lawyers rich.

Although Jim was angry when Jenna asked him to move out, they agreed to wait a year before taking any legal action. They continued to live in the same house and to hold their money jointly. One year turned into two, and by then, life had taken on a routine for everyone.

When Jim and Jenna decided to move ahead on divorce, they used a mediator to settle their financial affairs. They decided on a fifty-fifty split of assets, a fifty-fifty split on child support, and no alimony. Interestingly, New Jersey law required that each hire an attorney to advise them during the mediation. The lawyers created some tension as each insisted his or her client "could do better." In the end, Jim and Jenna ignored their lawyers' advice and made the deal they had previously agreed on. When Jenna remarried, Jim attended her wedding. When their son graduated from college, Jim and Jenna stood side by side to celebrate his accomplishment.

Parents who are planning to divorce ask how children will deal with going back and forth between two households. Will they think they are being abandoned? Will they ever forgive their parents? In the "Resources for Children" section in the back of this book and in the bibliography you will find material that will help you with frequently asked questions such as these.

As children adjust to divorce, they tend to mirror their parents' emotions. So the better you deal with the changes, the better the children will do. If a parent is stuck in anger, a child is likely to be stuck there, too. The same goes for the other emotional stages of divorce. Sometimes, however, the children appear to hold themselves together until the parents are on an even keel and then have difficulties after a routine has been established. Here are some difficulties and feelings that children experiencing their parents' divorce may have that you'll want to watch for:

1. *Acceptance:* Just like the parents, children will have trouble accepting that the divorce is really happening. They will

scheme to try to get their parents back together or secretly hope this will happen. They often do not give up this fantasy until they are about twelve years old and can begin to think in the abstract.

2. *Guilt:* Children of divorce commonly feel guilty and think the divorce is their fault. While this is never the case, many times the adult battles have been about parenting, so this feeling of guilt is understandable. Children may think that if they can be better, or be especially good, then the parents will stay together. Sometimes parents do blame the children, and it takes a lot of therapy or discussion to "undo" the guilt for them.

3. *Grief:* Children will need a grieving time just like the adults. Their entire world has changed and they experience much loss. The biggest loss is to no longer have the other parent living in the household. They may also have to change households, schools, location, and friends.

4. *Fear:* Children fear that if their parents can divorce each other, they might divorce the child, too. They need help understanding that the parents will always be their parents even if the parents are separated.

5. *Loneliness:* Children can feel lonely during a divorce. First, one parent is gone from the house, and then usually both parents are absorbed in grief. The child's needs may not be met as well as usual during this difficult time for the adults.

6. *Trust:* Trust will be impaired in children when their world suddenly changes from what it always was to something different. They may not know whom to believe if the parents tell them different things.

7. *Responsibility:* Sometimes a child must take on too much responsibility during a divorce and after. A child may be expected to help more around the house, take care of younger siblings, or even take care of the emotionally distraught parents.

8. *Caught in the middle:* Children may feel caught between the two parents. In contentious divorces, they may feel this even more so. Parents often use them as messengers, and they are usually in the middle of all the battles.

9. *Low self-esteem:* The self-worth of the child is damaged in the divorce just as for the adults. It takes some time for the children to reinvest in themselves and their new and different world.

10. *New families and new partners:* In many families, the child will also have to learn to adjust to a parent's dating, a stepparent, stepsiblings, and new family constellations. This is more difficult for them than most realize and takes a long time of work and healing and understanding.

If you are divorcing a narcissist, however, you are in for more than the usual difficulties of a "normal" divorce.

Divorcing a Narcissist When You Have Children

Divorcing a narcissist is a totally different ball game from getting a "normal" divorce. You might be in the same court system, but it does not work the same way. The narcissist does not play well with others. He or she does not necessarily follow rules, laws, and court orders. Unfortunately, you may find little support or understanding about what you are dealing with. Especially in the beginning, the professionals—attorneys, judges, parenting-time evaluators, and others—may assume that both of you are unbalanced and creating unnecessary and time-consuming problems. When you and your spouse cannot agree on such issues as custody and visitation, the professionals make recommendations and decisions for your children. You may be absolutely clear about what you think is in your children's best interests, but in contested situations, the courts make rulings about the children's "best interests." As many of the officials who help make these decisions may not be aware of narcissists and how they manipulate others, a court's sense of what is fair and in the children's best interests can be very different from your own sense, and you may even fear that the court's judgment places your children in danger.

One of the hardest things about divorcing a narcissist is knowing that your children will have to spend time with the narcissist parent without your being there to try to protect them. As I was writing this book, a heart-wrenching story was in the news about a father who had killed his three-year-old son after the boy's mother had been ordered by the court to hand her son over to his father for an unsupervised visit. The heartbroken woman said in an interview, "When we first separated, Dmitry told me that he would leave me alone only if I left him everything we had together. Money and assets were most important to him. Otherwise, he said, he would take the child away and I [the mother] will 'shoot myself from grief.' This was his sick way to take Kirill away from me."[5] Clearly this woman had to get out of that marriage and she had fought to protect her child, but the court did not recognize the father as the threat the mother had warned it about.

What happened to Kirill is an extreme example. Most parents don't fear that their children will be placed in physical or mortal danger when spending time with an ex, even a narcissistic parent. These parents are much more aware of the psychological damage the narcissistic parent can cause to the children. One of my clients told me, "I was taking my dog for a walk, and when we pulled into the parking lot of the trail, I saw a girl about age eight, riding her bike in circles around the parking lot. Her dad was on a cell phone screaming at the top of his lungs into the phone, 'You ____ing bitch. This is my parenting time. Why the eff are you calling me?' This went on and on with the worst vulgarity and screaming while the little girl just rode around in circles."

In plain English, my client was witnessing child abuse. Many states now understand that extreme verbal abuse by one parent of the other parent is emotionally abusive to the witnessing child. If this dad is acting so badly in public, what is he like behind closed doors? At a minimum this little girl will have post-traumatic stress disorder from being exposed to verbal abuse.

A colleague with a background in psychology who is both a divorce attorney and a parenting-time evaluator told me this about the effects on children of high-conflict divorce when one parent is a narcissist: "I have been doing this work for twenty-five years. I really have seen long-term emotional and psychological damage to children embroiled in ongoing conflict and bullying. I see them having low self-esteem and a difficult time with maintaining close relationships. I see some beginning to model their behavior after the behavior of the narcissist parent. Some even become abusive themselves as they get older. It is rare to see a child of these kind of cases come out unscathed."

With time and therapy, some of my clients have been able to put distance between themselves and their involvement with a narcissistic partner and move forward. My client Priscilla left an abusive marriage to save her son, Stuart, fifteen years ago. When she first entered therapy, she was severely traumatized. Recently, I ran into Priscilla and her second husband and was thrilled to hear that she is doing great. After the difficult, high-conflict divorce, she spent seven years as a single parent before meeting and marrying a man with two children. Her new husband had also had an exceptionally difficult divorce when his first marriage ended. Priscilla and her new husband are well suited to each other. They had some financial and parenting challenges with their blended family, but worked in partnership to address these. Eight years into their second marriage, they were holding hands as they walked down the street.

Priscilla's son, Stuart, is also doing well. He did have some difficulties during and after the divorce. It was tough for him to go back and forth between two very different parents who continued to have disagreements with each other. Priscilla said, "The thing that makes me happiest is that Stuart now has a serious girlfriend and he treats her well. It is a real, caring relationship with give-and-take."

Back to the Original Question: You Have to Assess What Is Best for the Children

In my practice, I see parents struggling with the question of whether getting out of a marriage to a narcissist will make life better or worse for their children. I also see adults whose narcissistic parents did or did not get divorced. If you have a narcissistic parent, you have been harmed by that experience and need to find a path to recovery. If you have a narcissistic spouse, your children will be harmed by that parent, whether or not you get divorced, and you will have to help them find a path to recovery.

The wounds are real. But one good parent who can give his or her child the priceless gift of good parenting with lots of empathy can make a world of difference to the psychological health of his or her children.

CHAPTER FIVE

THE DIVORCE PROCESS: COURT WARFARE

You might be at the very beginning of a divorce, smack in the middle of it, or struggling in the aftermath. No matter where you are, this chapter will give you a quick overview of how divorce works and the different professionals who may be involved. It will help you get acquainted with the challenges that you will be up against and show you that others are out there struggling in the same way you are. With this knowledge, you may get through a divorce more aware of the potential struggles and be better prepared to deal with them.

People in all lands and cultures struggle with narcissism, but the legal process of divorce that I describe here is that generally followed in the United States. Even within the United States, divorce works differently in different states. I have a good understanding of how things work in my home state of Colorado, but I am less familiar with the process in other states. As a mental health professional, not a lawyer, I will try to provide a mental health perspective to help you through the legal process of divorce.

Divorce is always difficult emotionally, but if you are divorcing a narcissist, the tricks that he or she will play on you to punish you for leaving and to keep you engaged in battle all make a difficult situation much harder. If you have no children with your narcissist partner, then you have less to fight about, which may make it easier to get divorced. Note that I said "easier," but not "easy." So, for example, if you are both relatively young, if you rent an apartment rather than owning a house, and if you don't own many assets together, then you may be able to get divorced relatively quickly, perhaps without involving attorneys at all.

Let's say that you do own a home or have shared financial assets. In that case, a narcissist may try to stay entangled with you by refusing to split property fairly and making outrageous claims about you in court in an attempt to discredit your claim on your shared assets. If this is the case, the challenge for you will be to strike a balance between getting out now and pursuing a settlement that is fair to you. I've had clients who said, "I needed to get out so badly that it was okay to let him or her have everything. That was the healthiest thing for me to do." I've had other clients who regretted not fighting harder for assets that were rightfully theirs. You have to decide which is of higher value to you, a fair distribution of assets or disentangling from this toxic relationship as quickly as you can.

Divorce with Children

If you have children, the number of ways the narcissist can manipulate you and prolong the divorce are many. Custody issues can become particularly contentious. In rare cases, the narcissist wants nothing to do with the children and doesn't put up a fight, but usually the narcissist parent uses the children as pawns in a battle to hurt you. Narcissists cling to their indignant posture of "How dare you do this to me!" They know you care most about the children so they use them to get what they want from you.

One client described her ex's frustrating behavior: "He didn't want the kids, really, so there was no fight over custody. We have a reasonable visitation schedule, but he doesn't always take his parenting time. It depends on if he has something better to do. He doesn't seem to understand the message this gives the kids. But, lo and behold, if I don't do something he wants, he immediately says, 'I will sue you for custody of the children and take them away from you.' He knows that's the only thing I care about."

Judges wish that parents could work out agreements with each other. When the parents can't agree, it's up to the courts to make a ruling. They do that by assessing the "best interests" of the child. This usually plays out in battles over custody and visitation rights.

Custody and Visitation Battles

Custody and visitation are a mess to deal with when a narcissist is involved. In many cases in my practice where parenting time is set, the narcissistic partner continues to go back to court over and over to try to change it by getting the court to order new evaluations. The court limits how often you can do this, but narcissists keep putting the children through more evaluations with new professionals, and their lives are disrupted again and again. Cases can go on for years, and the worst part is the damage done to the children, who are caught in the middle.

Tara had been married for twenty-one years and had three children when she and her husband divorced. She said, "We have been to court four times now and still don't have a parenting plan. He is manipulating the system and is doing whatever he wants to do. Our lives revolved around his business ventures, and I was not important enough to be able to work or go to school. I was expected to stay at home and raise our children, which I enjoyed. But at the same time, all of our finances were in his name and the business ventures' names. I was not allowed access to any of the marital assets. He bought whatever he thought we needed, and my needs or the children's needs were not met.

"He now believes that he built all of the businesses and that I am not entitled to anything that we have acquired in the last twenty-one years. He has kept our children from me during the two-year divorce battle, refused to pay taxes, licenses on vehicles, or bills because he thinks he is untouchable. My lawyer tried to make settlement offers that were just and reasonable, and he has only responded that he will not give up any money or custody of our children because he thinks that he will win in court. I am tired and out of money and am only praying now that the court will see through all this. I don't want the boys to grow up thinking that their father's behavior is normal or even acceptable. I hope that I can show them that there are much better ways to live and that men should be respectful and courteous to their partners. But what will happen to the parenting time? Will I get that chance?"

In a situation like this, Tara needs some trained professionals to help her. She needs to start by looking for another attorney who understands the toll this manipulation takes on her and the kids, and that new attorney needs to get a court order for a parenting-time evaluation for the children. Tara also needs a therapist who can help her with this stress. If her children are also in therapy, she should make sure that the therapist is aware of the issues that arise with narcissistic parents. A therapist who is experienced with narcissism can give feedback to the court and the evaluator on the children's needs and how they are adjusting to the divorce so far. Although being tired of the fight and out of money is a real problem for parents in this situation, going to court to battle this alone will not be as successful as it will be if she has a knowledgeable attorney and a new evaluation. This may be the time for Tara to try to borrow money from family or friends, or to explore other creative ways to find those funds.

Narcissists will seize on any excuse to bring you back to court to try to get the custody agreement changed. They watch for any mistake you make, as Sam recounted: "Anything that happens, my ex-wife tries to turn it into abuse. One time, when my stepson and our biological daughter were about nine years old, they were wrestling. My ex-wife found out about it. She stopped visitation and went back to court. She was found in contempt, but still this harms our family and especially the children. Another time, she decided she was going to move out of the country and take the children with her! I had to go to the Supreme Court on that one. It cost me about fifty thousand dollars. She only had to pay fifteen thousand dollars of those legal fees. Then her new husband wanted to adopt the kids and they wanted me to give up my parental rights. It just keeps going on and on. I have lost count of how many times we have been in court. We have spent at least one hundred thousand dollars now on this divorce."

Carey had been divorced for seven years but was still going to court with her former husband in a custody battle: "We've been to court seven times and there have been about four hundred and seventy filings to the court. There has been a cost of at least one hundred thousand dollars in legal fees alone, and that does not count all the evaluations and other professionals involved. If I had not had family members willing to lend me money, I would not have been able to protect my children. My ex went through six attorneys and eventually decided to go pro se and represent himself. Even when he had attorneys, he could not get along with any of them. He thought he knew more than they did. They also could not control him. He was mean to their staffs. In court when he is representing himself and he is asking me questions on the witness stand, it is a circus. He focuses on crazy things like asking me how much I weigh now and when I had my last drink. He would ask tedious questions about dates and times and averages, and everything I said got twisted by him. I felt it took the professionals a long time to really get what was going on. They need more training. We were both painted with the same crazy brush. You are damned if you do and damned if you don't, but you have to stay in to fight for the kids."

Brent also was frustrated with the court, unable to understand why it couldn't stop his wife from filing so many frivolous motions: "Mandy, my ex-wife, took me back to court at least every six months. There have been at least thirty motions filed, with legal costs way over one hundred thousand dollars now. She went through seven attorneys and then started representing herself. She would have emotional outbursts in court, and one time the judge even threatened to call the sheriff. She never followed court orders. It was like she felt she was above the law. She is constantly making allegations against me. Although none is true and none has been found actionable by the court, I can't tell you how difficult this has been for me, but mostly for our children."

While Brent cannot control what his ex-wife does or prevent her from taking these destructive actions, he should take care of his own mental health and that of his children. False allegations are harmful to children. Brent and his children should be working with therapists who understand high-conflict divorce and narcissism so that they can work to emotionally detach from this constant conflict. Brent may also need to file a motion, with his attorney's assistance, for a custody evaluation.

Evaluations Done Poorly without Regard for Narcissism Issues

You can see from these examples why it is important to have an evaluator who understands the dynamics of narcissism. Let's take a look at some of the problems that can arise if you are working with an evaluator who is not trained in the trouble narcissists can cause.

Most states have strict criteria and certify academic programs to train evaluators. Unfortunately many of these programs do not offer enough specific training on how to spot a narcissist or what to do if the evaluator is working with a narcissistic parent. Most professionals, including judges I've interviewed, believe more *specific* training is needed, which would teach evaluators how to recognize narcissism and how narcissists' aggressive and unreasonable actions harm their children, the long-term damage done to children, and how being raised by a narcissistic parent can affect a child into adulthood. Through this enhanced training, the evaluator will be aware of the consequences of allowing the narcissist to rage on unchecked by the courts.

A family law attorney, who is also a parenting-time evaluator, described his forty-hour, weeklong training to become a child-family investigator certified to do evaluations for parenting time. "There was actually little focus on abnormal psychology or psychological issues and particularly not on something as important as how to spot narcissism. Many of the people taking the training were also attorneys and not mental health providers, so they would naturally lack this important background. We needed this!"

The common myth that permeates the world of divorce professionals is that in a high-conflict divorce both parents are unstable and don't care if they hurt the children with revenge games. Yet it takes only one narcissistic partner to create a nightmare for years to come. If you don't have a seasoned evaluator who understands the narcissism dynamics, there will be problems. Clinicians can be seduced by narcissists, too, and I have seen this happen, resulting in more harm and lack of protection for the children. If this happens in your case, have your attorney submit a motion to the court requesting a new evaluator. If the court grants the motion, find an evaluator who you know is familiar with narcissism, someone who will not be swayed by the narcissist and can offer the court a better-informed second opinion. We will discuss how to choose an appropriate evaluator in the next chapter.

One mother, giving feedback about the evaluation system, said, "Even if the professionals seemed to understand some of this, they all said to stop the fight. That did not sit well with me because I had to fight to protect my child. The statement discounted me. It felt like another person telling me to stay helpless, like I had been in the marriage: 'You can't win, so give up.' Well, I couldn't do that to my child. Even though in the end I was not understood well and I got screwed financially, if I had not tried, I shudder to think where I would be today and my child as well. Many professionals just told me to take the attitude 'It's just the way it is and we can't change it.' Rather than saying how can we help to protect this child and help her to be more safe and comfortable, it was like they kept accommodating my ex and his needs came before the child. I lost many of the battles before the right things happened for our little girl. But, if I had not stayed in the fight, if I also had to feel like a failing parent who did not protect her child, I hate to think where the depression would have taken me. Sometimes I felt like the system was a replica of my marriage."

Having been trained as a family system therapist in marriage and family therapy, I was taught to look at everything in the context of the bigger picture. For example, if a child is acting out, look at the family system or the parenting. If the marriage is bad, look at both members of the couple and what they are each bringing to the table. In other words, hold everyone accountable. While this is common sense in many areas of psychotherapy, in some cases systems theory is not appropriate. For example, a blatant exception is when we have a sexual offender in the family. If a parent sexually abuses a child, the child victim is not blamed, the offender is.

There should be a similar exception for narcissists, who can unilaterally cause train wrecks with their selfish and often abusive demands, power and control issues, and manipulation to have things their way. They impose on others. Many seasoned and good therapists who are system trained may not have had specific training on how narcissists charm or manipulate others.

If the evaluators or other professionals do not understand narcissism, then the demands of the narcissistic parent may be met at the children's expense. While I am all for fairness, determining what is best for the children when one partner is a narcissist is something that takes skill and experience to evaluate properly. If you believe that your children are suffering because the evaluation has placed more importance on a generic idea of fairness to both parents than the happiness of your children, find another evaluator who understands the dynamics discussed in this book. In chapter 6, I give you specific questions to use to help you find an evaluator who "gets" it.

Jane described her trouble getting a fair evaluation: "We ended up having two evaluations for the children regarding parenting time and visitation. The first one was a seasoned professional, but he admitted he was afraid of my ex, told me he was a scary person and to be careful of him. I felt this evaluator could not be strong enough to protect the kids because of his own fear of retribution from my ex. The second evaluator was an attorney who kind of got it, but did not really see the impact on the children. She got seduced by my ex and believed his lies and she was manipulated by him."

Barry was frustrated by the system, too: "We ended up having two poorly done evaluations. The divorce has now cost over two hundred thousand dollars, and I doubt it will end until the kids are adults. We kept running into professionals who either didn't get it or were seduced by my ex-wife and her lies. She would feed the kids what to say when the youngest was only three years old. She ended up getting an attorney who bought all her BS, and even the marriage therapist didn't call out the affairs and her bad behavior. When I talked about my wife's behavior, the therapist only would say I have a right to my own opinion. I feel so sorry for my little girls."

I see cases like this often in my practice, and it frustrates me that the court system is often ill-equipped to handle the way narcissists maneuver around professionals who are trying to help the family reach an equitable settlement. Since Barry cannot get resolution in the courts, his best solution is therapy. The children need to be seeing a therapist who understands the dynamics of narcissism. As we will discuss later, the therapist cannot do parenting-time evaluations, but can testify about the emotional and behavioral effects on the children. Barry also would benefit from focusing on his own recovery work so he can continue to care properly for his children.

The Controversy over Fifty-Fifty Parenting Time

Evaluators and courts frequently award fifty-fifty parenting time in divorces involving children. Most people believe that children need both parents. I agree. Except in rare cases of extreme abuse, children should continue to have both parents in their lives. However, in working with hundreds of children of divorce, I have seen that fifty-fifty parenting time is usually not workable for children. Children who are living the daily reality of fifty-fifty typically complain of having their weeks disrupted by having to pack things up to go back and forth between households. This is true even when both households have good parents. Children need a stable base, a place to call home, just as adults do.

When one parent is a narcissist, fifty-fifty parenting time will not work well because it requires constant communication, respect, and empathy for the children's needs, which narcissists lack. In these cases fifty-fifty is an ongoing nightmare for the children, with long-term harmful effects.

A family law attorney that I interviewed commented, "The pendulum has swung to fifty-fifty parenting time, but the current research is not showing it is working. I think there is a good chance this will be changing back to one parent being the majority-time parent. With a narcissistic parent, and fifty-fifty, I don't think our system limits their parenting time. I think they see it as the child needs to learn to deal with the limited-capacity parent, too."

One prominent judge I interviewed was also skeptical of the fifty-fifty arrangement: "I don't have a solid presumption of fifty-fifty being best for kids. I like to see the case first. You have to take into consideration the ages of the kids and the involvement of the parents historically. In a narcissistic parenting case, they don't always have a bad relationship with their kids. If I think it will reduce the conflict, I may lean in that direction."

Although I totally get cutting down on conflict, there has to be a better way!

David Bolocofsky, a family law attorney who also has a doctorate in psychology, had a different view: "I don't necessarily believe that fifty-fifty parenting time is always best and for all children. To some extent, it depends on whether there is equal bonding and attachment with the children. With a narcissistic parent it is substantially inappropriate. Lack of empathy is a primary problem. When one party is a narcissist, the fifty-fifty will usually not work. An equal time-share may not be in the child's best interest and can be a ticket to disaster. Empathy is at the core of competent parenting, and by definition narcissists have an impairment in empathy."

The more seasoned a professional is in dealing with narcissists, the more appropriate his or her evaluations and court orders will be for the kids.

A few years back, I worked with a three-year-old boy whose parents had a court-ordered fifty-fifty parenting schedule. The father was a diagnosed narcissist. The mother had dropped her son off for therapy, and according to the parenting-time schedule, the father was supposed to pick him up.

When this little boy realized that his father was going to pick him up from therapy, he began to throw himself on the floor and against the wall, screaming, hitting himself, and kicking. He was unable to express his distress in words. This went on for fifteen minutes. When his father arrived, the boy tried to hide in my office. The child was having difficulty with staying overnight with his father, but this was a court order. Although a new evaluation was soon to begin to review the parenting-time schedule, at this point I could not help this child.

Sometimes as a child therapist I feel desperate in these cases. What can I do therapeutically when the system is allowing this to happen to young children?

In this case I found a way to help. The child's mother and I discussed this problem with her attorney, and I spoke with the new evaluator about the child's emotional state. I also continued to work with the child so that he could learn to express his feelings in words. Eventually I hope to arrange a father-son session where the child can begin to speak up about what he is struggling with emotionally when he is with his father. Continued work with the mother will be important as well to help her learn how to calm her son and help him express his feelings at home, too. Learning these skills is important for all parents who share a child with a narcissist. I will say much more about empathetic parenting in chapters to come so you will have tools to help your child.

A father whom I interviewed shared a heart-wrenching story involving his two young daughters. The visitation schedule was limited for the narcissistic mother as the father has primary parenting time.

The children had not had contact with the mother for about a year due to her substance abuse and concerns of child endangerment. But after an evaluation the mother was ordered to do individual therapy specifically to work on her addiction issues and empathetic parenting skills.

The father described how his ex-wife's therapist focused more on her as an individual and encouraged such things as yoga, meditation, and breathing techniques, instead of working on her addiction issues or parenting skills. "This seemed to increase her inflated sense of self," the father said. "Then we had to move forward to try to reunite her with the girls. My ex-wife's therapist said that she was not a real danger to the children, and so the court ordered us to begin transitioning from supervised to unsupervised parenting time. When I sent the girls on their first unsupervised visit, they came home hungry, tired, and dirty. I asked them how it went, and their response was 'Can't we send Mommy back to therapy? She doesn't know how to take care of us.' My ex is going back to court for more parenting time and is totally oblivious."

One time I was testifying in a difficult case of this sort. I recommended that the narcissistic parent get some coaching for empathetic parenting. After I recommended a particular psychologist to do the coaching, the judge asked, "Doctor, what would the parenting coach do, really? Bring the dad in and tell him to be nice to his kids and then what? And I know that psychologist you recommended. . . . What will he know? He doesn't even have kids!"

This judge's comments showed that he did not understand the skills and training that are required to become a psychologist, nor how therapists can help people to change their behavior. We needed the judge to hear what the children needed, yet it seemed that he already had his mind made up on the way this case should go. When you face a judge who is not sensitive to the issues that come up with a narcissistic partner, the best route, as I have suggested in earlier examples, is to assemble a team of professionals who are experienced with narcissism. If many respected professionals report to the judge their assessments of the case, chances are better he or she will look at this additional information and find a way to intervene that will be more helpful to the child and to the family.

Court Orders Not Followed: Ding! Rounds Six—
Seven—Eight

Even after thorough evaluations have been conducted and court orders clearly laid out, narcissists continue to cause trouble. They don't obey the court orders and drag their former spouses back to court. If they don't like the answer, they seek further action. They don't just settle down and get on with life.

A prominent, seasoned judge told me that when he sees these cases, he knows he has to make his orders more detailed so that they micromanage everything about the couple's lives with their children. "I have a sense of frustration: no matter how hard I work to make a detailed, ironclad order, they will be back," the judge said. "They keep litigating. I've seen cases with five hundred and seventy-one pleadings in one case. We call them our 'frequent filers.' Then some go pro se and file their own pleadings, and we have a series of contempts and modifications for minor violations of the law. They feel they are entitled to this or that, and the amount of judicial time it takes is out of proportion to the normal cases. After a while we know what sports the kids play, what schools they go to, and all the ongoing minutiae. The frequent filers are here every three to six months at least. We usually can't limit this. Restrictions are hard to impose as our authority to do so is limited. You have to find they are being abusive in the filing and the judicial process. But the worst is that they don't realize how much they are hurting their children. I eventually see this impact of the conflict and the litigation. I see kids doing worse in school, bed-wetting and displaying anxiety, rebellion, and many of them brainwashed and under the control of the narcissist, aligning with the narcissistic parent for their own safety."

A client in therapy shared this story: "My ex-husband likes to prove he is above the law. He will take amounts of money he owes me and leave off ten or twenty dollars just to make his point. Not enough money, of course, to take it back as contempt as it isn't worth it financially, but just enough to drive us crazy. If he is supposed to pick up the children at a certain time, he is either late or forgets or tries to change it each week so nothing is predictable. I always feel he is in some secret planning mode and the other shoe is about to be dropped. It is hard to feel safe even now after five years of divorce. The children can't get used to this. They try to make excuses for him, but I can see their hurt every week."

When court orders are not followed regarding money, visitation, and property settlement, this disrupts the normal development of the children. Narcissists also tend to disparage the other parent even when the court says again and again that this disparagement is a violation of the court order. As my client Mandy described: "My ex was told over and over not to disparage me directly or indirectly to the children. But he does it all the time. They come home from visits saying, 'Who is right and who do I believe? Daddy says the divorce is your fault.' He was also ordered to not say things like 'Do you love your mom more than me?' but he interrogates them constantly. In order to protect themselves, they have to give their dad the answer he wants, but then they end up so very confused and upset. He continues to tell me that he will fight me till the day I die and eventually the kids will hate me. He tells the kids all the time that I am messed up!"

Mandy is describing the distorted view of the world so common with narcissists. As a parent, you will need to learn how to validate your child's feelings without also disparaging the other parent. This is not easy, and it requires a lot of discipline to resist defending yourself to the children, but being defensive places the children in the middle of the argument, which is bad for them. In chapter 9, on helping your wounded children, you will learn more about what to say to your children if their other parent is a narcissist.

False Allegations

Some divorced narcissistic parents will use any misstep or lapse by the other parent—such as a scraped knee, a childhood illness, or a drop in the child's grades—to drag the parent back to court. One attorney called these the "diaper rash" cases. Sane people work together to coparent and don't expect the courts to handle all the day-to-day struggles of raising children.

To convey a lie through a child in order to hurt the other parent is a form of severe emotional child abuse. In many cases children are told to convey a lie made up by the narcissistic parent and are coerced into making accusations against the other parent. Narcissists ask their children to repeat lies about physical, emotional, and sexual abuse when nothing else is working for them.

Because narcissists focus on taking revenge in a divorce, they do not see the harm they are causing children when forcing them to repeat a false allegation.

The worst is when narcissistic parents tell their child that he or she was sexually abused by the other parent just to try to get more parenting time. It is heart-wrenching to do an evaluation with young children who tell you a parent did something to them sexually and they can't remember it but the other parent told them about it. Of course many allegations of child abuse are true. I have spent my entire career working on abuse cases, and I am not quick to assume an allegation is false, but all allegations must be carefully assessed. When evaluations find the accusations to be false, we see amazing relief in these little ones who have been told to carry the lie. They say things like "My dad kept asking me over and over and over if I was touched on my privates, and so I just said yes to get him to stop."

In one case the narcissistic parent hired a therapist to interrogate her son. This therapist actually told the child he had been sexually abused by the other parent although the son had no memory of this and loved the other parent. If your ex alleges abuse in your divorce case, your must hire professionals who are specifically trained to evaluate trauma in children. This specialized field requires much extra professional training. Don't assume that all mental health providers have this training.

Kids' Activities and Needs

I often say to people in therapy that putting a roof over your child's head and giving him or her food to eat and clothes to wear is not parenting. A child can get that in an orphanage. Tuning in to your child's emotional world is parenting.

Children are busy little people with school schedules and lots of activities to manage. Our job as parents is to help them explore the world, develop their skills, nurture their emotional growth, and learn how to go handle the difficulties of life. Narcissistic parents not only don't help their kids learn to deal with their own lives, they expect the children to cater to the self-centered adults. As Michael said, "My ex-wife was all about herself and her own needs. Our son was in college and he was really busy. My ex could never understand this. I remember my son calling me one time just to vent. He told me that his mother had called and e-mailed him over fifteen times in a twenty-four-hour period. I can't even remember what it was she wanted him to do. Tim had a full schedule of classes, sports, and community service, and his mom expected him to drop everything and make her priority his top priority."

Narcissists have no ability to understand the emotional welfare of children. They do not have the capacity or the understanding. Narcissistic parents do not support the activities of their children unless those activities are interesting to them. If the children's activities interfere with the narcissist's game plan, the children often have to give them up. Many times, children just give in to please the narcissistic parent. They become defeated.

One eleven-year-old told me, "I used to play soccer and I loved it. We had practices and games and I had friends there, but I had to quit.

The schedule didn't work with my dad's parenting time, so he would not bring me. I think he was just lazy and also trying to get back at my mom, because now that I quit the team, we don't do anything at his house but watch television or go out to eat. I miss my friends."

Nine-year-old Hannah told me, "I was in gymnastics and on a fun team. I have been competing since I was six, and it is my favorite thing to do. But now we have meets and some of them are a ways from home or even in other towns. I never want my mom to take me. She is too busy to think about breakfast, my outfit, my snacks, or anything that helps me. At the meets, she wants to leave right after I compete. She doesn't understand that I want to cheer my friends on and stay for the whole meet. But the worst thing is, my mom wants me to quit because she says it is too much work for her. What am I going to do?"

Holidays

Holidays are special to children. Most parents want to make holidays fun and memorable for their children and share traditions, love, and gift giving. For narcissistic parents, holidays are just more opportunities to battle rather than work with their exes as sane parents. The holidays often get ruined for everyone in families with a narcissistic parent.

One father I treated called his children on Christmas Day while they were at the mother's house for the holiday. "I called and asked to speak to my kids to wish them a merry Christmas. My ex-wife answered the phone and said, 'This is my parenting time and you are not talking to the kids. Do not call here again. You are ruining my holiday.'"

Narcissists fight about visitations, the exact times for drop-off and pickup, money, gifts, and camps.

Chris told me that, after her divorce, "Christmas was no longer any fun for the kids. They don't like the back-and-forth between households and the fighting over the time. My ex always waits until the last minute after we have made our plans according to the parenting plan and then asks to change times right before the holiday. Last year, I just said no. I am following the parenting plan. So, his revenge was to not see the kids at all. They did not understand this. Their dad didn't see them at all with any gifts and they had no idea why. I knew it was because he did not get his way and this is how he punishes me."

Chris had to explain to her children that their father was struggling with some problems of his own, and to say this in a way that did not disparage their father. Her therapist also instructed her to make sure she listened to the children's feelings and validated them. While this is a good approach to handling these disappointments, soothing words by one parent can only help so much. If these kinds of situations continue, the children should be in therapy to assist them to find their own ways to heal the damage inflicted by the narcissistic parent.

Dealing with Bullies

Dealing with a narcissist in a divorce is like dealing with a bully. The wear and tear you will experience when you try to protect your child's emotional welfare will be significant. Even though you are mentally healthier than the narcissist, you can look unstable to the professionals involved in your case due to your reactions to the bully's abusive behavior. Let's compare your divorce to a high-conflict bullying situation on the playground. Michael Friedman, in an article for *The American Journal of Family Therapy*, describes a scenario in which a child is repeatedly attacked by another child to provoke a fight. When the teacher steps in to break it up, he hasn't witnessed the beginning of the fight so he blames both children. Understandable in some ways. The teacher could spend a long time trying to establish who instigated the fight and might not ever be certain. "But to the child who was provoked and who finally responded, being seen as an equal participant in the conflict and being punished is a miscarriage of justice."[1]

This happened to my own son in junior high school. One day, I got a call from the principal, saying he was going to have to do an in-school suspension of my son. The principal told me that an older kid kept pushing my son's glasses off his nose and shoving him. My son reportedly kept walking away and trying to ignore the kid. The principal and a teacher had both observed this behavior. I was proud to hear that my son was following my advice to fight his battles with his head, not his fists, until the principal described how my son had finally had enough and threw a big punch that hit the kid so hard it caused a nosebleed. The principal told me he wished my son had knocked out this kid! Wow! But they both got suspended.

The bullying is "vulnerability in self-esteem," which makes narcissistic people very sensitive to 'injury' from criticism or defeat. Although they may not show it outwardly, criticism may haunt these individuals and may leave them feeling humiliated, degraded, hollow, and empty. They react with disdain, rage, or defiant counterattack."[2] At the crux of the narcissist's problem is a fragile self-image. If narcissists are abandoned in a divorce, they don't get over it. It lingers for years while they continue to use the children as a way to stay connected with the ex-spouse and to maintain some kind of control. Their internal dialogue may sound like this: "No one breaks up with me!" Or when the narcissist leaves and the ex gets involved with another person, the narcissist thinks, "I don't want you, but I don't want anyone else to have you either. How dare you!" This perceived slight can turn into narcissistic rage. And the bullying behavior continues.

I know of a family in which the four adult children in their forties are still being affected by their narcissist father's grudge against their mother from a marriage that ended some thirty years ago. To this day, this father refuses to be in the same room with the mother. He won't allow the children to speak her name in his house. When the children started having children of their own, the mother came to the hospital for the births. When the father showed up, he insisted that the mother had to leave. The same issues came up at weddings, graduations, and funerals. In all normal life activities the children continue to suffer in order to protect themselves from the narcissistic rage of their father and disparagement of their mother.

A woman posted this anonymous response to an article on my *Psychology Today* blog about divorcing a narcissist: "My husband's ex-wife was a serial cheater and for the past ten years has continued to vilify and drag him to court. That has been her vehicle to act out her rage at his divorcing her. Most people would never be as sadistic as to ensure a court motion awaits in the ex's mailbox on their wedding day! That is the lovely gift we got on our wedding day! God help the poor men who end up with these damaged beauties.[3]

We usually see some bad behavior from people during a divorce; we expect that. But using the children as pawns or continuing the retribution for years is inexcusable.

The Cost of High-Conflict Divorce

When high-conflict divorce involves a narcissist, the costs can be outrageous. In cases where the families do not have a lot of money, narcissists cause havoc in other ways, but adversarial actions involving custody and visitation can cost from $50,000 to $1.2 million.

Sadly, some of our best-trained, seasoned, and experienced people are leaving the field due to retribution from narcissists who file lawsuits and grievances with licensing boards to ruin the reputations of these qualified professionals.

One seasoned parenting-time evaluator, who asked not to be identified, told me this story: "I have been doing this for so long, I have had over a hundred lawsuits and grievances filed against me. I am used to it now. I will tell you, with some of these cases of extreme narcissists, though, it can be frightening. I drive a bulletproof car and carry a concealed weapon."

Another parenting-time evaluator observed, "Retribution is extremely common with narcissists. It is rare that we do not see retribution. They file against all of us if we don't agree with them. It is accurate to say that this kind of thing has driven out some very capable professionals from this field. It affects their malpractice insurance and drives them out. It is very unfortunate."

I had an intimidating experience in my office with a narcissistic father whose children were terrified of him. I was trying to explain the importance of empathy for his children, which he didn't like hearing about. He stood up and, talking smack in my face, grabbed both of my forearms, saying, "Don't you get how *you* are hurting my kids?" Thankfully, when I took a step back and quietly asked him to take his hands off me and leave the building, he did comply.

Fear of these kinds of encounters keeps many clinicians who could be of assistance to children and parents out of the field of divorce work. Many young therapists I talk with and those I train say they are afraid to work in this field because of the risks of retribution.

The Adversarial Legal Battleground

Our court system is set up as a legal battlefield with both sides trying to "win" their case. But in divorce with children, the lives of the children need to be more the focus. The children need to win.

Many family law attorneys work hard to stay out of the conflict between the parents to do what is best for the children. But some attorneys encourage continued warfare as more conflict results in more money for them.

An attorney friend recently remarked, "You know how people say that when a couple has been together for a long time, they start looking like each other? It is like narcissists tend to find narcissistic attorneys who are like them and enjoy the battlefield and the ongoing warfare. If the lawyer engages the same way as the narcissist, you are going to have trouble."

One of my friends who recently got an amicable divorce told me that although she and her ex were able to settle most things, including arrangements for their only child, they were both amazed at how the lawyers did everything they could to get them to be at each other's throats. They tried to convince my friends that the other would steal money and encouraged alimony and a court battle. She says if she had listened to the lawyers, she does not think their child's best interests would have been served.

Another attorney friend summed up the problem: "There's no question to me, as a lawyer, that the narcissist who acts 'normal' with an acute and overdeveloped sense of his or her entitlement to special treatment, who can lie in a cunning way, has a distinct advantage in court disputes. They usually find lawyers who want to believe their lies and fuel their narcissistic supply. The court battles become fun for them all. It is a place to perform and win. Then the judge, who is trained and retrained in neutrality, has to weigh the claims of the effective liar in as serious a manner as the person responding to the lies. The system is supposed to sort out truth from lie, but persistent, effective lying frequently sweeps the battlefield. At the very least, it multiplies the costs of litigation."

Who Can You Find to Help You?

Now that we have looked at the many problems with these kinds of complicated cases, we will move to helping you find the resources you need. The next chapter will discuss the various professionals in the divorce field and what you should be looking for to help your family.

CHAPTER SIX

Getting Help: Troops to Defend You

As you go through a divorce, you have to work within the current system, but that doesn't mean you have to be at its mercy. You can do lots of things to make the current system work for you and your children. In this chapter, I will talk about reaching out to the professionals who can help you get through a divorce. These troops will do battle for you and your children. I will also tell you how to build a support network of friends and family. While giving you some general advice on finding the right attorney, remember I am a mental health professional and cannot give legal advice.

What Kind of Professional Help Do I Need?

You need to hire an attorney and find experienced therapists for you and your children. If you anticipate a court battle over parenting time, you will want to work with a professional who specializes in parenting-time evaluations.

Attorneys

In recent years, with the economy in recession, more people have tried getting "do-it-yourself" divorces in which they fill out the paperwork needed and present it to the court for an order. Usually divorce packets can be purchased at your county courthouse for a minimal price. This can be a sensible thing to do if the divorce is simple, with no children, little property or assets, and no question of alimony or maintenance. However, if your spouse is a narcissist, then he or she has a history of being able to manipulate you, so an attorney will likely be able to represent you better than you can represent yourself. Most divorce cases do settle out of court, but unfortunately those involving a narcissist don't.

You want to avoid your spouse's having an attorney and you not. As one Texas judge said in a recent interview about do-it-yourself divorces, "When a person without a lawyer is divorcing someone who has an attorney, it can complicate the divorce for the party without legal representation."[1] This judge noted that people who represent themselves may, for instance, have difficulty following the proper legal procedures to be sure that the judge hears their story.

The right attorney for you and your family is a family law attorney who has significant experience with divorce cases, who is attuned to the problems of emotional and/or physical abuse, who is experienced in advocating for children, and is someone you can trust. You have to do your research to find a solid family law firm. Some attorneys claim they do everything . . . but family law, just like mental health, is specialized.

The websites of (or other information from) law firms will give you great examples of how they view divorce when children are involved. Some things to look for are:

1. Do they blog about high-conflict divorce?
2. Do they mention experience with narcissists or difficult cases?
3. Do they blog about children and protecting them?
4. Do they say anything on their site about the best interests of children?
5. What do they list as their specific practice areas?
6. Do they mention anything about your specific needs as in the children or property settlement?

7. Do they seem to present with empathy, such as mentioning something about divorce being financially and emotionally traumatic?
8. Does the site say anything about child custody?
9. Do they seem accessible and easy to understand and contact?

You may also get leads from online articles such as the one titled "The Psychological Impact of Divorce on Children: What Is a Family Lawyer to Do?" This Baltimore attorney, Kendra Jolivet, suggests specific actions that family lawyers can take, working within the current system, to help children, including:

• Providing a letter or pamphlet(s) to the client with resources (schools, organizations, churches, etc.) that offer services to children going through divorce.
• Requesting "best interest attorneys" for the children in high-conflict divorce cases so the voices of the children can be heard by both parties and the court.
• Suggesting therapeutic and educational options such as parent education, peer counseling, group counseling, men's and women's groups, individual counseling, coparenting, and family therapy.[2]

Besides searching on the Web, you may get referrals to an attorney who is competent, caring, and knowledgeable about both legal and psychological issues from family or friends who have been through divorce. Go to your local state bar association website and search *family law attorneys*. Read the specific information about their background, credentials, education, specialties, and how long they have been in the field. Searching their individual websites will give you insight on cases in which they have been involved, and articles they have written about their special interests and expertise. You should have this information before you begin to interview an attorney for your case.

A good rule of thumb is to interview at least three attorneys before making your decision. You will want to go prepared with a list of questions like the ones below. If you have not been involved in legal cases before and have not worked with lawyers, interviewing them will give you a good idea of the differences in style and approach so that you can choose an attorney who fits your criteria. You are looking for someone who treats you with courtesy, respect, and caring.

When you are looking for a divorce attorney, it is normal practice for attorneys to give you the opportunity for an initial consultation. The initial consultation allows you to meet and interview the attorney, describe your situation, and find out how the attorney practices. Some attorneys do free initial consultations and some don't. Seasoned and experienced family law attorneys will generally not have time to give free consultations. It will be worth it to pay for their time because you will get more valuable information this way.

The attorney should start by asking you questions about yourself, your spouse, and what your concerns and priorities are. The attorney should be easy to talk to. Do your best to evaluate if the attorney seems genuinely interested in you and picks up on statements that characterize your spouse's narcissism and your concerns about your children. Even though many attorneys may not understand the dynamics of narcissism in families, they will be used to working with difficult people.

After you've asked about the attorney's retainer, how much he or she charges, and how you will be billed for work, ask the attorney more specific questions like:

- How long have you been in practice?
- What areas do you specialize in?
- Do you have a philosophy about how you approach divorce cases?
- Are you concerned about children's issues?
- My spouse is a narcissist. Can you tell me if you are familiar

with narcissism and explain to me how you see it, and what concerns you might have about this divorce?

- My spouse is emotionally abusive to me and my children. Do you have experience representing people who have been emotionally abused?
- Do you work with or recommend therapists in divorce cases?
- How do you interact with children's therapists in these cases?
- What experience do you have with child-custody and visitation disputes?
- Do you have a point of view on what kind of parenting-time division is best for children?
- What is your feeling about joint custody versus single custody when a narcissist is involved? Or, what is your feeling about fifty-fifty parenting time or joint decision-making?
- How do you communicate with your clients?
- What steps would I anticipate in the divorce?
- What has been your experience in dealing with any cases that are similar to mine?
- How many times have you been in court?
- How many times have you been in court in my county and where my case will be filed?

Joint decision-making is important to discuss with a potential attorney for your case. In Colorado, divorce provisions are made for where the children will live, for visitation schedules, and for how the parents decide on such issues as the children's education, religion, medical treatments, therapy, sports and extracurricular activities, and other practical issues. If you are awarded joint decision-making with a narcissistic spouse who does not act in the best interests of the children, you will have continuing difficulties with your ex until the children are at least eighteen. You may not be able to get around this, but in general, the cases I have seen in my practice where one partner is a narcissist, the joint decision-making does not work well.

If joint decision-making has been awarded and is not going well, you may need to go back to court and change the parenting-time arrangement. To prepare for this, it is helpful to keep a daily diary of the behavioral and emotional issues the child or children are having. If it involves grades or school, talk to the school personnel and get their input as well. If the child is manifesting physically with medical symptoms, you will need the notes from the pediatrician. Your child's weekly visits to the therapist will give you a good assessment of the changes in the child's behavior as well as what the child is saying about the issues.

You may want to keep a calendar of events that the children attend and record on the calendar the issues that come up surrounding each event and how the child reacts to those.

If verbal abuse of you or the children is ongoing, recording conversations to give to your attorney or evaluator can also be helpful. I would only do this if the verbal abuse is serious, as most evaluators do not have time to listen to many recordings. You might have to select a few for them to hear to make your point that the problem is serious.

In initial meetings with a lawyer, you may be asked to bring in copies of financial information so the attorney can give you a sense of what your rights will be in the settlement of property and other financial issues, such as child support and maintenance. While you want a lawyer who will be a strong advocate for you, you do not necessarily want to retain a pit-bull lawyer. California attorney Thurman W. Arnold III, certified family law specialist, explains, "People enmeshed in divorce tend to think that they should hire the most aggressive divorce attorney they can afford. Some lawyers market themselves to respond to such values and this impulse . . . [but] hiring an attack dog is a recipe for disaster. It is like saying the only way to settle an argument is with a fistfight. . . . When lawyers act upon our clients' deepest hurts and self-interested desires, when *normal people* [emphasis added] are scripted to hire a junkyard dog to get what they think they want, need, or deserve, it becomes a lose-lose situation."[3] Attorney Arnold said he believes that people benefit from finding a collaboratively trained lawyer even if they don't have a collaborative case.

You need to be aware of the likely implications of your attorney choice. If you hire the most aggressive divorce attorney you can find, you are guaranteed to have a fight. On the other hand, you do need an attorney who will be appropriately assertive in representing your interests.

If you have significant estate or property issues, or know that you will have difficult financial negotiations, you will want to find an attorney who is not only a specialist in family law, but one who understands business and estate law as well. If you or your spouse own a business that will have to be evaluated, which can be complicated, your attorney will need to work with specialists who can do this properly.

Most family law and divorce attorneys have worked with mental health professionals, but some have not. It is important to find out if a prospective attorney is comfortable with hearing from your mental health professionals about what is going on in your family.

If abuse is part of the reason for your divorce, you may also need to find out if the attorney works with private investigators. Well-connected law firms work with specialists to help build the best case for their clients and negotiate the most appropriate settlement.

Find out if the attorney has worked with the judges in your county and also with the parenting-time evaluators in your community. What has been their experience, good and bad? Some evaluators in my community are known to be either "for the fathers" or "for the mothers." In my view, either leaning is wrong because good evaluators should be for the children.

You don't want an attorney who loves the fight and will carry on a case forever. You want one who is reasonable and a good person and interested in settlement. The attorney's job is to advocate for you in the best way he or she can, not to keep the battle going. Your narcissistic spouse will likely find the "fighter" brand of attorney who is unreasonable and acts just like the narcissist, so you need a reasonable attorney to try to move the process along in an orderly way. In my experience, judges respond better to the reasonable attorney than to the attack dog.

As the divorce proceeds, you will have to document everything. Begin this right now. Begin with keeping a file of all the legal papers. Keep them organized and in chronological order. Also get a notebook in which you can record dates and times of any abusive events your ex perpetrates on you or the children. Be sure to record as well the emotional reactions of the children to the narcissist's bad behavior. Also keep a record of the issues that are arising in simple interactions such as picking the children up or returning them, taking them to doctors' appointments, and disputes over vacations and holidays. Most people are emotional during a divorce, which makes it easy to forget important things that you will need to tell your attorney. If you keep careful records of things as they transpire, you will have all the facts you need for a court hearing or evaluation.

Some states have organizations called Legal Aid that represent people for free or for less money than private attorneys charge. If you are limited on funds, this may be something to look into as well. The waiting period for representation may be long in some states as these free services are much in demand. In some states, Legal Aid will only represent families if there is documented child abuse or spousal abuse. Colorado, for example, has a Denver Bar Association legal clinic and an organization called Metro Volunteer Lawyers, which assist those who cannot afford private attorneys.

Some attorneys will work with you to keep down the cost of litigation by asking you to do a lot of the legwork and research while still acting as your consulting attorney and representing you in the courtroom or in any legal paperwork presented to the court. This is sometimes referred to as unbundled legal services. Attorney Stephanie Kimbro explained that in unbundled legal services a law firm breaks down a legal matter or a client's legal needs into components. "The attorney tells the client that as your lawyer I'll handle certain parts of your legal matter and you are responsible for the other parts of the matter," she said. "So with an unbundled legal services agreement you must define very clearly the responsibilities of both lawyer and client."[4]

Some couples try getting the same attorney to oversee the final paperwork, but usually that attorney will only represent one of you officially.

The Pros and Cons of Mediation

The definition of mediation is "an attempt to bring about a peaceful settlement or compromise between disputants through the objective intervention of a neutral party."[5]

Thurman W. Arnold III, CFLS, shared his mediation philosophy: "Being a mediator is a metaphor that speaks to our desire to live whole, meaningful, and generous lives. We are blessed with an invitation to redeem our personal stories in the course of helping others, and thus to live more wakefully in the present. The disputants who share their conflicts with us offer a path to such open-heartedness. Those we hope to lead themselves remind we facilitators that each one of us lives fully only in relationship with others. That is their great gift to us in return for our efforts, and one reason why we are drawn to this practice.[6]

For people who are not about the fighting and the power and control, mediation can be helpful, and a healthy way to resolve disputes for the family. It is just not likely with the narcissist. A narcissist's perception of reality is that their way is the right way, so they are not usually able to use mediation or to compromise. Mediation with a narcissist is usually difficult and most times not worth the expense. I hate saying this because mediators are generally trained to be more like peacemakers who are drawn to helping people resolve conflict instead of continuing the chaos of the adversarial struggle.

One interviewee told me, "We went to a mediator for free, but they told me they found my ex too difficult to mediate with so they called it off."

Another client said, "The mediator actually told me to ask my child what she could do to not make her father so upset. I was shocked that she wanted our daughter to be responsible for keeping her dad happy."

Another person interviewed shared this story about his mediation experience: "I watched my ex at work. I watched the mediator actually change her mind about the facts of the previous mediation meeting. It was fascinating. I watched my ex-wife change her tone, cadence, and expression with this mediator, and before I knew it, the mediator had begun to agree with everything my ex said."

Darin told another failed-mediation story: "We were constantly in mediation. That's what everyone advised. But, within the first couple of months, the mediator threw up her hands and said you will have to take this woman back to court!"

In Colorado, the courts often order mediation before the first court hearing in hopes that the couples will settle their differences there. Some states have government-sponsored mediation programs, and some involve attorneys and mental health professionals. This is different from one state to another. You will have to research what the process is in your community. You may also want to look into private mediation services and models called collaborative law.

If the laws of your state compel you to try mediation with your narcissistic spouse, take your attorney with you and document the manipulation and power and control tactics. When mediation fails, as it almost always does when one of the partners is a narcissist, your records will describe what happened in the negotiations before mediation, and how mediation did not solve the dispute. Your notes should describe the behavior of the narcissist, how he or she acted in mediation, and that there was no compromise and no consideration for the welfare of the children.

Finding a Therapist for Yourself

The divorce is going to be hard for you. You've been trapped in a relationship of distorted love. Deciding to pursue divorce does not magically break you free from that sticky web. Your spouse has always been good at manipulating you, and you need help to break that pattern. A therapist can also help you in many practical ways, such as to:

- Work through your emotions and the trauma related to your marriage in a safe place.
- Establish and enforce new boundaries.
- Understand how your spouse has been manipulating you and how to defend yourself against manipulative tactics.
- Begin developing a healthier sense of self.
- Develop your own empathetic parenting style, a style that will help your children to develop into healthy young adults.
- Decide which battles to fight.
- Support you through the divorce.

If you have never seen a therapist, you may not know what to expect from therapy. Some folks have had a bad experience in therapy and decided not to try it again. Let's discuss what to expect from a seasoned mental health professional.

A trained therapist will get to know you, your individual background, and any traumas you have experienced. When you are divorcing a narcissist, you need to find a therapist who understands the dynamics of narcissism in intimate relationships. This may be more difficult than it sounds, so be sure to ask about this when you are searching for a therapist. Your therapist should also be familiar with the court system and divorce procedures and have had experience testifying in court. While there is no guarantee you will need this, you would want a therapist who is not afraid if your case calls for this kind of testimony.

I believe therapy has three general components. The first part helps you learn about yourself, your background, your history, your family of origin, and your issues, coming into the present day. The second part is working toward healing and recovery with the feelings examined in the first step. When this part is done well, it is then possible for you to move to the third step, where you begin to reframe your experience and see things through a different lens so that you can move on in your life.

That is a lot of ground to cover, so you and your therapist should begin with a plan with specific goals for your therapy that you both agree to. When choosing your specific goals, assess what you think you need the most assistance with. It may be your grief, helping the children deal better with the divorce, how to deal with your ex, assessing your communication skills, assessing how you are or have been manipulated, working on your new life as a single person and parent, or working with your new financial challenges. These are just some examples. These goals may change as you go forward, and the therapist may also identify some areas in which you need additional help.

The most important aspect of therapy is the relationship that you will develop with your therapist. The mental health field calls this relationship the "therapeutic alliance," and it means that you have developed a strong and trusting connection with your therapist and feel safe to be yourself and ask for help.

Maybe you can't find a good therapist in your town or can't afford to see a therapist. That does *not* need to stop you from charting your own course of recovery. Here's how I think about it. A therapist can help guide you through the difficulties of divorce, but in the end, you are the one who has to walk the path and do the work. Therapy should not be a forever commitment. You may find it helpful to see someone just a few times. If you cannot afford to go to a private therapist, check your local mental health centers, as they provide sliding-scale fee services.

In chapter 8, I give you a road map to recovery, along with specific tools you can use on your journey.

Finding a Therapist for Your Children

A child therapist who is trained in understanding the dynamics of high-conflict divorce and its impact on children will be able to help children deal with not only the divorce, but also the parent who is not emotionally attuned to them. The therapist must understand the impact of narcissistic parenting and how this can have long-term effects on children. Such a therapist can give your child tools to deal with that parent, tools the child will use for a lifetime. Feelings, fears, divorce loyalties, changes in his or her life, custody, and visitation issues will all be discussed in the child's therapy. When it works, the child therapist's office will become a place where the child feels safe to discuss important feelings about the family that he or she may not feel comfortable discussing with parents during this complicated time.

A narcissistic parent may cause disruption in your child's therapy, but even a brief experience with a good therapist can have a big impact on a child who is trying to make sense of his world. For instance, one adult survivor described his experience: "At one point the court ordered psychological testing for all of us, because my mom said my dad was manipulating me into lying. I saw a psychologist five times, under the court order, and then my mom tried to sue the therapist because he wouldn't release my records. She even tried to bust into a session and had to be escorted out of the building. Then he wasn't allowed to see me anymore. It was a good thing being able to see him, and having to terminate after five sessions was a shock. I really wanted someone to rescue me. It let me have that fantasy. The last time I saw him, it really changed my life. He explained why he had to stop seeing me. He gave me a suggestion for a helpful book to read. I still remember his name."

We will describe in more detail what you need to consider when hiring a therapist for your child in chapter 9, the chapter on healing your wounded child.

Child Family Investigators and Parenting Responsibilities Evaluators (Colorado)

In Colorado, the judge can order that your family be assessed by a child family investigator (CFI). CFIs must have a professional back-

ground in either mental health or law, and they take a forty-hour training course to be credentialed as CFIs. The state prohibits them from
charging more than $2,000 for their evaluations, and their expert-
testimony charges are also capped.

The CFI assesses your family situation efficiently and without too
much intrusion to make recommendations to the court on issues that
affect the best interests of the children. The CFI investigation does not
include other assessments such as drug and alcohol testing, psychological testing, or child abuse assessments.

If a more detailed assessment is needed, it is wise to pursue what
is known as a parenting responsibilities evaluation (PRE), a more detailed and expensive assessment. These assessments take longer but
may be worth it in the long run in dealing with a narcissist. In Colorado many of our PRE evaluators have extensive experience in custody cases. You will need this kind of evaluation when dealing with a
narcissist who wants to battle in the courtroom, but who is not particularly aware or concerned with the best interests of children.

What Does "Best Interests of the Child" Mean?

Most states believe it is important to have a parenting plan that allows children frequent contact with both parents. The court rarely
terminates a parent's rights, usually only in cases with documented
physical or sexual abuse. In just about every case, your ex is going to
have significant time with your children during and after the divorce.

If you and your partner do not agree on custody and visitation, or
you want the court to be aware of certain problems, frequently the
court orders an evaluation of the family conducted by a trained professional like a CFI or a PRE. Although these evaluations may have
different names in different states, every state uses a "best interests of
the child" standard for custody disputes or disagreements.

The following, for example, are the physical, mental, and emotional conditions the state of Colorado evaluates to determine the
child's best interest:

1. The parents' living environments and situations, including the financial stability of the parents.
2. The parents' psychological health or mental health issues.
3. Any prior domestic-violence or child-abuse issues.
4. The developmental age and needs of the child.
5. The prior history of parenting with each child.
6. The bonding and attachment of the child to each parent.
7. Sometimes, the children's wishes or preferences if the child is sufficiently mature to express a reasoned and independent desire.
8. How each parent supports the other parent in their relationships with the children.
9. The wishes of the parents.
10. The child's adjustment issues related to home, school, and community.
11. The physical health of the parties involved.
12. Practicalities related to the physical proximity of the parties to each other.
13. The ability of the parties to put their child's needs above their own. (I particularly like this one!)
14. Sibling relationships.[7]

If you are seeking a court-ordered parenting evaluation, you or your attorney must submit a motion to the court. Typically lawyers on each side submit names of possible candidates to the court, but sometimes the judge simply picks an evaluator whom he or she knows to have a good reputation. An experienced family law attorney will be aware of evaluators in your area who they know do a good job, but they may not be familiar with those who specialize in serious psychological issues such as narcissism. It is important to find professionals who understand a narcissistic parent's impact on children. Make sure to tell your attorney that you need someone on your case who is experienced in these issues. It is a good idea to research the evaluators in your area so that you have some names to give your attorney as well.

Here are some questions to ask to ensure that the evaluator is appropriate for the issues unique to a divorce from a narcissistic spouse.

Evaluator Questions

1. Credentials.
2. Experience in the mental health field.
3. Experience with parenting-time evaluations or custody work.
4. How many evaluations have they done?
5. What kind of training did they receive to be able to do this work?
6. Do they have experience working with children?
7. Do they have experience working with the specific ages of your children?
8. Are they familiar with child development and what is important for children at different stages of their growth?
9. Are they capable of assessing personality issues and do they typically give psychological tests in their assessment? Or do they hire it out if needed?
10. How do they bill for the evaluation and what is their cost?
11. How do they typically conduct the evaluation? What procedures do they use?
12. Are they familiar with narcissism and how it plays out in parenting and relationships?
13. Have they worked with a narcissist before?
14. Do they know how to spot a narcissist?
15. What is their general feeling about fifty-fifty parenting time if one of the parents is a narcissist?
16. Have they worked with abuse cases? Emotional, sexual, physical?
17. Do they like to talk to the therapists involved in the case?
18. How do they give you feedback at the end of the evaluation?
19. Do they have experience testifying in court?
20. Have they testified in your particular county before?

I believe it is best that the attorney or paralegal interview the evaluator rather than for you to do it yourself. You don't want to give a wrong impression to the evaluator, who might begin assessing you from the kinds of questions you ask. I have seen this happen.

This court-ordered parenting evaluation is designed to assess both parents and the full home context to ensure how to serve the children's best interest. This can become another battleground in trying to make an agreement with the narcissist. As stated earlier, the narcissist will want to find the "best" evaluator in town, with the "best" credentials and the most prestigious university background. Also you may be concerned that your narcissistic spouse will manipulate the evaluator: "Will my narcissistic ex-spouse charm the pants off the evaluator?" "Will the evaluator 'get' the issues?" "Will the judge understand?"

Jack described how much he worried about this when divorcing his wife, Julie Ann, whom he feared could charm anyone. "She did it to me, she does it at work, and she is good at it. She will lie and manipulate to get what she wants. She loves to emasculate me to anyone who will listen and even to the children. She recently told the kids that I am not a good father and that is why she is divorcing me. If this were true, that's one thing, but I know and the children know it is not. I am emotionally connected with all three of my children and spend a lot of time with them. Julie Ann is a controller and controls them with an iron hand, they are afraid of her, but they don't talk to her about their feelings. They do not show her any vulnerability. I have had to be the psychological parent since birth and gladly so, but they really missed something here with their mother. Now she is saying she will get full custody and parenting-time decision-making and I will be left in the dark. I am terrified for my children that the evaluators will not see through it. She is good at this!"

As part of the evaluation, the custody or parenting-time evaluator will interview each parent separately, usually at home so that the evaluator can assess the home environment. He or she may ask the parent to play a game with the child, make dinner, or do something interactive so the evaluator can see how the children and the parent relate to and interact with each other. The evaluator will also interview the children.

The evaluator will review all the court documents and records to date, including any abuse allegations. He or she may contact those who know the child and the family such as teachers, child-care providers, therapists, pediatricians, and sometimes friends or family members. In some cases, the evaluator might do psychological testing of both parents or use other questionnaires to provide additional information about the parents' mental status or parenting skills.

The final report will have a summary of all of the evaluator's findings and will also make recommendations on parenting-time and decision-making arrangements for the parents. The judge may or may not follow these recommendations, as the ultimate judgment on these matters remains with the court. The judge usually writes a detailed parenting plan including many specifics, right down to the fine points of sharing of holidays and school breaks.

If there is much disagreement, which there will likely be with a narcissist, the evaluator may also recommend that a post-divorce parenting coordinator assist with big decisions that may become stumbling blocks. The parenting coordinator may be given power by the court to make some decisions so that the case will not go back to court if the parents continue to disagree.

The evaluator's report sometimes also recommends therapy for either or both parents and the children. Note that since these evaluations are part of the court record, they are not confidential.

If There Are Child Abuse Allegations

If there are child abuse allegations in your case, you may also need to find a CFI or a PRE experienced in assessing child abuse. Make sure to check that your prospective evaluator has dealt with abuse cases. Many times evaluators will refer out to specialists for abuse assessments and incorporate those assessments into their final reports. My office is sometimes hired just for sexual and physical-abuse evalua-

GETTING HELP: TROOPS TO DEFEND YOU

tions of children or to evaluate children who are sexually acting out. We submit reports to the PRE. The professionals who specialize in abuse assessments know how to interview children without asking leading questions and understand how to assess the credibility of the child's statements. They are also trained to look for signs of the child being coached by either parent.

Building Other Support Networks

This book is written to help you chart a course to healing. Chapters 8 and 9 are all about healing yourself and your children. You may also find it helpful to reach out to others to build your support network.

If your narcissistic partner was also an alcoholic or a drug addict, you can gain wisdom from 12-step programs such as Al-Anon, which is free. It has also been interesting to me to discover how many people who have a narcissistic partner have turned to what one woman I interviewed called "Google therapy." She said, "I could not understand what was happening in my marriage. I was so isolated, and I didn't really have friends or family that I could talk to about it, so I started googling. I googled things like 'my husband talks about himself all the time' or 'my husband lies all the time' or 'my husband seems to cheat' or 'my husband can't be alone.' I just started googling things I was experiencing and started coming across all these pages that talked about narcissism, and it just crystallized for me. It made sense. When I figured out he was a narcissist, I was relieved to be able to put a label on it. I devoured anything I could find about narcissism. Then I started posting questions on some of the sites, and people answered me. They were supportive and understood where I was coming from. It was amazing."

I, too, have been impressed by some of the caring and thoughtful comments that people have posted on my own site and on others. At their best, some of these sites feel like good group therapy, where you can gain phenomenal insight from people who have had the same experience as you. However, Google therapy has some real limitations. It's not private, it's not individual, and it's not typically run by professionals. It's also not therapy. You can find people online who are not interested in true recovery but want instead to just vent and keep things stirred up. This can lead you down the wrong path at times, so choose your online groups carefully.

While giving you some general guidelines in this chapter on finding the right professionals to help you, the third part of this book will be addressing specific recovery for you and your children if you are divorcing a narcissist.

PART THREE

Healing from the Debilitating Impact of Narcissistic Relationships

CHAPTER SEVEN

POST-DIVORCE COMBAT: RAISING YOUR INTERNAL DEFENSES

The men in my family are duck hunters. I have pictures in my head of them crouched in camouflaged duck blinds and other quiet spots in the country, waiting for the ducks to fly over so they could take them down, one by one. Unfortunately, I also have this same image in mind when I think of narcissists: they wait, plot, and scheme for revenge and the final win in situation after situation. They don't stop and they don't get over it.

So, you need to come up with your own game plan to protect yourself from the shots your ex is going to take at you. This chapter will discuss practical strategies and give you coping tips for everyday post-divorce life, and parenting after divorcing a narcissist. I will keep this separate from your healing process as these are two different things. This chapter is about dealing now, in the present, with the realities of your situation. In the next chapter, we will take the healing inside for your own recovery. In the end, all you have control over is your own thoughts and recovery.

Once the divorce proceedings are over and life is moving on, you will still have to engage with your narcissistic ex because of the children. This will be true for many years to come, so you need coping strategies as you coparent. You may be thinking you just can't do it or you don't want to do it, or you have no idea how this will even work, but it can, when you raise your internal defenses consciously and concertedly.

They Don't Give Up the War: Narcissistic Injury Revisited

To defend yourself effectively and navigate through life after the divorce, you have to understand more about the psychology of the narcissist you are dealing with. We discussed the psychology of narcissism earlier in the book, but will revisit it here briefly as it is so important to understand. When narcissists feel that they have lost or they feel rejected or abandoned, they don't forget it. We have all felt abandoned or rejected at times in our lives, and most of us get over it with a little time and processing of the feelings. We move on. But the narcissist does not do this. Narcissists are not enough in touch with their own feelings to move on. The issues remain in their mind as "It's all your fault." "How could you do this to me?" They want to strike back and often do it through the children.

Narcissists suffer from what the *Diagnostic and Statistical Manual of Mental Disorders* defines as narcissistic injury: "vulnerability in self-esteem which makes narcissistic people very sensitive to 'injury' from criticism or defeat. Although they may not show it outwardly, criticism may haunt these individuals and may leave them feeling humiliated, degraded, hollow and empty. They react with disdain, rage, or defiant counterattack."[1]

While they may act arrogant and haughty and put on a show that nothing bothers them, this façade makes it difficult for you to see their inward self-loathing. You may be thinking, "Are you kidding me? She thinks she is the hottest thing on earth and no one can measure up to her!" But as they do not have a solid, developed sense of self, narcissists swing from depression to grandiosity with little in-between. Their presentation deceives most people until they get to know the narcissist. When the narcissists' façade of charm and deception gets cracked, their whole world bursts apart. They will blame you for their feelings of inadequacy, lack of happiness, lack of love—even after the divorce is made final.

Jerry shared this observation about his ex-wife: "I honestly thought my ex, Mary, was one of the most confident people I had ever met. She was a competent professional in her field and made good money. Her house was immaculate all the time. I wondered how anyone could be so perfect in so many ways. But as time went on, I noticed how envious she was of others, how competitive she was, how she always had to come out on top no matter what it was . . . discussions, arguments, or anything we did. She had to be the winner. And if I ever commented on something that she interpreted as criticism, it seemed like she never got over it. She would bring it up over and over and never let it go. It is like she would 'clock' it somewhere in her brain and couldn't forgive or forget. It would be over dumb things, too, as I would never be critical really. But, for example, she would ask about something she was wearing, and if I said I liked a different outfit because of the great color on her, she would interpret it strangely and make up her own explanation that was never correct. 'Oh, you think I am trying to be too sexy in that, I suppose. You think I dress like a whore.' I would be totally floored by her interpretations. I now understand better that she had very low self-esteem that she worked hard to mask."

Understanding how the narcissistic injury works will help you be better prepared for post-divorce parenting. In your marriage, you have already seen the different behaviors that arise when the narcissistic injury is triggered. However, it gets worse when narcissists are feeling rejected or abandoned in a divorce and leads to another behavior, called projection, that is also important for you to understand.

What Is Projection and How Do I Deal with It?

In traditional psychoanalysis, *projection* is a term used to describe a type of defense mechanism "in which intolerable feelings, impulses or thoughts are falsely attributed to other people."[2] We can all project our inner feelings onto others at times. If you are tired or stressed, or out of touch with your feelings, you may attribute the source of those feelings to someone else—your kid or a coworker or boss—and blame that person for how you feel. However, you will likely realize what you are doing, stop it, and recognize that you're responsible for how you feel. Narcissists take projection to an extreme. Let's look at some examples of how this works not only in a relationship with a narcissist, but even after the divorce is final and you are coparenting.

- The narcissist begins to lose interest in you. Rather than admitting his own emotions, he will say, "I don't think you like me anymore."
- The narcissist is thinking of infidelity. Instead of owning her own feelings, she accuses you of cheating on her.
- The narcissist is being a bully but accuses the person he is bullying of being a bully so he can feel better about himself.
- The narcissist is experiencing jealousy but instead accuses you of being jealous of her.
- The narcissist has done something wrong, maybe even illegal, such as spousal abuse or child abuse, but instead he makes you the villain and accuses you of the bad behavior.
- The narcissist is angry at someone, but accuses that person of being angry at her.
- The narcissist hates his job and wants to quit, but tells you that you want him to quit his job. You are making it difficult for him to continue. You are to blame.
- The narcissist decides she does not want to be with you for some event but she projects her feeling onto you, saying, "You don't want me there, anyway!"
- The narcissist files one motion after another to keep your divorce case in court but projects this onto you, saying, "Look at what this divorce is costing me because you are not reasonable!"
- The narcissist does not honor parenting time with the children and instead chooses to do his or her own thing, such as golfing or being with friends, but projects this onto you, saying, "You are keeping the kids from me and I don't have enough time with them!"

- The narcissist agrees to a financial settlement, but after the divorce constantly tells the children it is your fault that he or she has no money.

These are only a few examples of how projection works. You can see why you may have been confused as the narcissist's partner if you didn't know what was going on. Projection is a relationship killer. Narcissists use it to feel better about themselves and to release themselves from accountability. They continue to use projection to try to manipulate you after the divorce is final.

As an adult you can understand what is going on when you see this happening, but children cannot. When a narcissistic parent projects bad feelings onto a child, the child will tend to believe the parent and will internalize or accept this negative message. This is emotionally damaging to children.

Don't Take It Personally

When you understand projection as discussed above, you learn not to personalize a narcissist's messages and can more easily step back from these tactics. You know it is something going on inside the narcissist, and therefore you don't have to take it on. You can help your children to disregard these messages, too.

Cecilia described that it took her a long time to understand that the problems she was having with her ex were not her fault. "He was like a snake in the grass, camouflaged, cunning, and it was so hard to detect what he was doing until I got away from it. Then I'd come back and see it, and then as the days go by, it becomes camouflaged again. Crazy making. It made me forget how to live, basically. I have to remind myself even to this day that I am not dealing with a normal, rational human being. You still expect certain responses and comprehension, but I am not dealing with someone normal."

Brent described it briefly but vividly: "It is so easy to be sucked into her vortex of craziness and then have to defend yourself or justify. She could pick and pick at me, and it would tear me down to a pale state of depression and feeling of incompetence. Learning to not personalize this and know it really was not me took a long time of healing."

Remind yourself before, during, and after any encounter or exchange with a narcissist that the narcissist's views are not true, they're not about you, they're about his or her distorted perception of self and the world. Take a deep breath, count to three, and see yourself separate and apart from these projections.

How Do I Truly Disengage?

As you coparent after divorce, you must still engage with your narcissistic former partner, but you can disengage emotionally from the battles. When you are enmeshed inside the narcissistic web, it is more difficult to separate from the strange things that happen. Once you are separated or out of the marriage, you can see that you are not wrong and it is not your fault. Your goal is to get to the place where you are standing outside of the craziness and looking at the narcissist's behaviors more objectively, separating yourself from his or her projections and distorted worldview.

Your Own Triggers and History

If you were raised by a narcissistic parent or come from a narcissistic family, you will likely find that certain actions, phrases, attitudes, and experiences in the present spark unexpectedly strong emotional reactions because they remind you, often unconsciously, of people or episodes that harmed you in the past. Mental health professionals call these triggers. Recognizing your triggers and knowing what sets you off can help you be less reactive. Let's look at some examples of triggers and what can happen.

Jessica never felt loved by her narcissistic mother, which left her with a nagging feeling that, if her own mother couldn't love her, then maybe no one could. Jessica told me, "I always felt like my mother did not know how to love really. She sometimes said the words 'I love you,' but rarely showed affection or tuned in to me as a child. It was really all about her all the time. She told me that I would never find a man to love me because I was such a difficult person. She was obsessive about my weight and my hair, and I could never please her. I was never good enough for her. So, when I got married, I had this nagging feeling that my husband didn't really love me, but instead would leave me at the first opportunity. I walked on eggshells. I didn't realize that I had gotten into a relationship with a narcissist and had actually married my mother, much to my dismay! But I was easily triggered if I felt abandoned in any way during the relationship."

Since Jessica felt emotionally abandoned by her mother growing up, her fear that others would abandon her, too, was her trigger. If she felt her husband was not tuning in to her feelings, or if he threatened to leave her when she did not do exactly what he wanted, she would experience intense fear and sometimes have panic attacks. Despite these fears, Jessica had a hard time disengaging from her ex. She continued for years to try pleasing her husband, as she had her mother, to no avail, and then would constantly feel "not good enough." Through therapy she recognized this cycle and took steps to end it and to end her relationship with her ex.

Bill had not had a secure attachment with either of his parents. He said, "I could never trust them as they did not follow through on promises and rarely acted like they knew the real me. They wanted me to perform all the time for their self-aggrandizement, but didn't really care about my feelings and how things felt to me. I think this caused me trust issues with love relationships, and I can get easily triggered around trust. I generally mistrust people until they prove to me at great length that they can truly be trusted. Even though I married a narcissistic woman, I think I brought some trust issues to the relationship and need to work on that."

When Bill's ex demanded high performance without consideration of Bill's feelings or desires, he would get upset with her. Much like Jessica, he felt he had to please his ex anyway. For example, once, when his ex wanted the yard to look perfect, with no weeds and everything in order, Bill was exhausted from a long week of work. Bill found it difficult to set boundaries for himself and tell his ex that he was too tired and the yard work would have to wait until he got some rest. He did the yard work just as she had insisted he must. The legacy of having been raised by narcissistic parents was that he felt he had to perform or he could not trust his wife to still care about him.

Carolina had a similar experience to Bill's: "In my family of origin it was all about what you did and not about who you were. It was a high-achieving family so you had to be on your game, performing and achieving, or my parents did not approve. How you looked, acted, and whether you won was the mantra for our family, so it was exhausting to always be onstage like this. I think it caused a certain kind of perfectionism in me that could get triggered easily if I felt I was not measuring up somehow in my marriage. If the house was not clean enough, or I did not weigh the right amount, or my clothes were not great, or I was not achieving big-time at work, there was hell to pay and I kind of bought into it. My narcissistic husband played into my triggers big-time and used it against me by constantly judging and criticizing me. I had to give it up in the end, but I know these triggers made it more difficult for me. How great would it be to have a relationship with someone who was into healing with you and not just stomping you into the ground?"

No one grows up in a perfect family. There are no perfect parents. We all bring some baggage to our relationships from our past. The key is what we do with our issues and how we heal ourselves. Having a trigger or problem from your past does not make you a narcissist. But it does mean you may have recovery work to do from having such a parent as well as from having a narcissistic partner.

Your Internalized Messages

In researching *Will I Ever Be Good Enough? Healing the Daughters of Narcissistic Mothers*, I found that women had internalized negative messages based on how they had been treated by their narcissistic mothers. You may have internalized similar messages based on your love relationship with a narcissist. This is also true if both of your parents were narcissists and does not only apply to women. It is important for you to be able to identify these messages so you are aware of your sensitivities. The most common ones are:

- I feel unlovable.
- I feel never good enough.
- I feel empty.
- I have crippling self-doubt.
- I feel valued for what I do rather than for who I am.
- I don't trust my own feelings.

All of these internalized messages can get triggered when dealing with a narcissist, and you can feel depressed or angry. For example, if you internalized self-doubt from your upbringing with a narcissistic parent, when you are insulted by your narcissistic ex, it is easy to doubt yourself again rather than trust your gut or intuition. If you felt unlovable growing up with your narcissistic parent, and then again with your narcissistic partner, it is easy to believe that no one can love you. If you have always felt valued for what you do rather than for who you are, you need to work on valuing yourself now and giving yourself credit for your character and personality, not just for what you are achieving. Becoming aware of these internalized messages will help you to disengage from your narcissistic partner.

What Are Boundaries and How Do I Set Them?

A boundary is simply drawing a line in the sand that represents what you will do and what you will not do. Note that narcissists typically do not have good boundaries around themselves, nor do they like boundaries set on them. We all have our limits, and it is important for your mental health to know what yours are and when the narcissist is crossing or ignoring them.

Narcissists feel they are above the law, so personal boundaries are easy for them to violate. Maintaining a solid line in the sand many times means hanging up the phone, turning off the phone, walking away from situations, closing doors, driving away, and other such tactics to enforce your limits.

Setting boundaries does not have to be done in a hostile manner. With practice, patience, and restraint, it can be done with courtesy and kindness.

Let's look at some practice dialogues:

Your ex says: "I left some things in the garage and I am stopping by after work to get them."

You say: "I am at work today and it is not all right with me that you just stop by my house anytime or enter my garage. You will have to schedule a time to do this when it works with my schedule. You must respect my schedule or I will contact law enforcement about your trespassing."

Your ex says: "I know I was supposed to be there at six p.m. to get the kids, but I am coming by after school instead."

You say: "We are going to follow the court orders exactly, and you cannot change the times at your whim. The children will not be at the house after school because we have other plans. We will see you at six p.m. as planned."

Your ex says: "You sure don't know how to take care of a yard. It looks horrible. I can see how you must miss me doing that."

You say: "This is my yard and I will take care of it." (Do not engage in these kinds of battles at all.)

Your ex says: "I don't really have the money for child support this month, so I will make it up next month."

You say: "We have court orders that you must follow so that the children are taken care of. I will expect the payment or I will be contacting my attorney so we can set up taking it from your wages at work. I am not willing to play this game even one month."

Your ex: Swears at you on the phone and is verbally abusive.

You say: "I will not allow you to speak to me that way any longer. Just so you know, each time that you do this, I will simply hang up the phone." (Hang up. Do not engage or fight back.)

Your ex: Disparages you in front of the children and you hear it.

You say: "This is not good for the children. I will remove them from this situation and I will speak with them about why it is not okay for you to do this. They will be told this each time you are determined to put me down in front of them. I won't disparage you, but I will let them know that this behavior is not acceptable."

Your ex: Sends disparaging and abusive e-mails frequently.

You: Ignore them, but do save them or send them to your attorney. (Do not engage in fighting over e-mail.)

One client told me this story about his narcissistic ex-wife: "I was one of those codependent types with her in the marriage. I always took care of her and everything, and we all had to orbit around her to keep her happy. She still tries to get me to help her even though we are divorced. It is really interesting. She will constantly ask me to pick up her cleaning or go to the grocery store on the way over to pick up the kids. I just learned how to set boundaries with her and just say *no*! It feels really good."

Think about the boundaries that your ex tries to cross. Write out some of the situations in your journal. Now think about possible responses, such as those I've given you in pages 116–117, that set and enforce your boundaries. Practice setting these boundaries in your mind until you need to use them.

Communicate Clearly

Clear communication is important with narcissists because they have a distorted perception of reality. They can twist your words. To communicate clearly, use *I* statements that own your feelings and language. This is in contrast to using *you* statements. When we point a finger and begin the sentence with *you*, it comes across as blaming. We are basically backing someone into a corner, and when the person has no place to go, he or she comes out punching. We can't expect narcissists to validate or acknowledge what we are saying, but we can at least clearly state where we are coming from.

Some examples of this follow:

Rather than say . . .	Try . . .
"You make me uneasy."	"I feel uneasy about this situation."
"You are not hearing me!"	"I feel unheard in this conversation."
"Stop swearing at me!"	"I am not comfortable with this conversation."
"You are making me furious!"	"I am feeling angry and need to go now."

You can see how owning your feelings and statements enables you to communicate clearly and keeps you out of the blame game. We feel what we feel. Feelings don't have brains, so someone cannot argue with our feelings. But if we do the blame game, the battle continues.

A common type of communication in narcissistic families is triangulation, in which one person speaks to a third party in hopes it will get back to the one for whom it is intended. This indirect way of communicating is damaging and hurtful. If you find yourself caught in triangulation talk with the family, simply say you only speak directly to those you have messages for and you will not pass things through other people. If someone gives you the information, you simply state that you prefer that he or she communicate directly to that person.

This triangulation becomes a serious problem when the children are used to relay messages to the other parent. This position is heartbreaking for children to be in. Children should not be the messengers between battling parents. Do not allow this to happen. When your ex does this, don't take the information and explain that the other parent should only talk to you directly and the children do not need to give you messages. We will explore this further in chapter 9.

Don't Justify Your Actions

When engaging with a narcissist, you are often on the defensive because of the narcissist's constant criticism and negative judgments of you. But you can make a statement about what you are doing or feeling without having to justify it to anyone. We do want to justify and explain ourselves to some people, but with narcissists justifications only give them more room for criticism. Often your explanation starts an argument. Use your *I* statements and let it stop there. If asked why you are doing something, decide if it feels appropriate to explain further, and if it does not feel comfortable, don't go there.

For example:

Your ex says: "What were you doing last night? I tried to call you and you did not answer your phone."

You say: "I was busy and I am sorry I missed your call. I am calling you back now when I have the time to do so."

Your ex says: "The kids say you are eating out a lot and not cooking them meals at home."

You say: "When the children are in my care, it is my responsibility to feed them, which is what I do."

Your ex says: "I heard you were dating someone. How dare you do that so soon?"

You say: "My personal life is my business."

Be Accountable but Don't Expect Accountability Back

Being accountable for your feelings and actions is a must for sound mental health. There is nothing wrong with apologies when they are in order; it feels better to own your mistakes when you make them. This is true even when someone has been ugly to you.

Let's say you got overwhelmed and you just lost it in a conversation with your ex. You yelled at him or her or said something mean. To be accountable is to say, "I am sorry about how I handled that conversation, and I will work on keeping my emotions under control. I want for us to have an amicable situation, and I do not want to add to the problem by allowing my anger to come into the situation with you. I may be angry but I know it is not okay to use name-calling and yelling."

Your job is to follow your value system even though you are dealing with a narcissist, and a trademark of narcissism is lack of accountability. Narcissists are not likely to own their actions or behavior unless those actions make them look good. You should set a higher standard for yourself. If you feel that you have said or done something wrong or hurtful, make a point to be accountable. This will make you feel better in the long run, and it also models appropriate behavior for your children.

It is your responsibility to model good behavior for your children, because a narcissist cannot. They learn more from what they see than from what you say. Even though you know your child will learn some bad behavior from the narcissistic parent, you will have to offset that by being a good role model. It is what I call double duty. Not fair, but it is what it is. It is another way to disengage from the narcissist. You can teach your children how to deal effectively with difficult people if you don't use the same tactics that were used on you by the narcissist. You don't have to be mean back.

If your ex is mean or ugly to you and calls you names in front of the children, this does not mean you have to do the same. You can merely make assertive *I* statements about your feelings and back out, walk away, turn off the phone, etc. You can say you are not comfortable with being treated disrespectfully, but you do not have to engage back with name-calling, yelling, and frustration. When you walk away, you are modeling what you would want your child to see and do.

How to Deal with Manipulation

Narcissists are masters at manipulating people by throwing temper tantrums and getting into rages. They also use power plays and control tactics, such as withholding money, attention, and affection if they do not get their way. They may sometimes even try to sugarcoat their manipulations by acting nice or doing something for you. They always follow up a seemingly kind act with more manipulation, however. For example, your ex offers to bring dinner over for you and the children on Saturday night, but you know that he is trying to be especially nice because he wants to change visitation for an upcoming trip with the children. Allowing yourself to be manipulated has to stop. First you must sort out the ways the narcissist manipulates you. Often there's a pattern. "When she did this, I usually did this. When he said one thing, I followed with another." Take some time to figure this out, so you are not caught up in more of the same. Using assertiveness and self-empowerment will help.

For example:

1. Your ex uses anger or rage to try to manipulate you. You are afraid of the anger so you typically have given in when it

comes at you. You now realize this and don't engage in the argument and walk away. You use your *I* statement to say that this is not okay for you now.

2. Your ex uses sugar or something nice to try to convince you of something he or she wants. You bought this in the past because you so wanted some kindness in the relationship. You now realize it is just manipulation, and you say, "No, thank you."

Pick Your Battles

Narcissists don't forgive and forget. They love to win. They have to be on top and make everything a struggle. When coparenting, you will have to pick your battles carefully with your ex. Some things are not worth fighting over. At times you have to sit down with yourself and ask how important this issue is to you. If you can live with it, and it means you don't have to engage, let it go. Someone cannot fight with you if you are not willing. Most people learn this the hard way.

Say your ex wants to change the visitation time for one event that is going to cause you some inconvenience, but it does not affect the children in any adverse way. This might be one of those times when you decide to let your ex get what he or she wants without objections from you.

Maybe your ex's parents are in town and he or she wants to change the visitation schedule to accommodate their visit. This may not be worth fighting about if it falls during your scheduled time with the children. You can let it go and make up your time with the children later.

Or perhaps an awards ceremony involves your ex and he or she wants the children to attend, even though it falls in your parenting time. If it is possible just to let this one go, you can save your children some grief, as this is one less battlefield in which the children will get caught.

If Your Ex Adds a Stepparent or Significant Other

Your ex's romantic life is not your business, and you have to let it go. The only place you get involved is when you need to explain something to your children. If you do, you do it in a factual, noncritical manner. The addition of other people into the family mix is common, and you will do this eventually, too. You hope that your ex will choose someone who is kind to your children. That should be the most important factor to consider. Know that you cannot control this. Let it go. Pray for the best and deal with what comes.

For example, if the children tell you that your ex is dating someone new, you may be angry because you have seen that the kids are upset by the new parental dating scene. Do not disparage your ex or criticize the choice to date. You simply explain to the children that after a divorce the parents usually do start dating again, and you are there to help them with this adjustment. Also explain that this is something children cannot control, but you care about their feelings and you will always talk with them about this.

Perhaps the children have a new stepparent whom they don't like. They complain to you constantly about this new person. Your job is to listen to the children and validate their feelings without disparaging the other parent or stepparent. If the situation feels abusive to you, you may need to talk to your ex about this, get the children in therapy to discuss it, or, if it's bad enough, speak to your attorney or parenting-time evaluator.

The main point for you is that you cannot control your ex and what he or she is doing in his or her personal life. But you do need to protect your children at all costs.

Children eventually figure all this out. Getting them through all the adjustments in the beginning of parental dating is difficult. Your job is to not bring someone new to the picture until the children have gone through their own divorce adjustment, which usually takes two to three years. You may casually date, but give yourself and the children some time to adjust. But your ex . . . you can't control.

The Digital World of Communicating with a Narcissist

The digital world of communicating with the narcissistic ex has its ups and downs. With the advent of texting, e-mails, Facebook, LinkedIn, Twitter, Skype, FaceTime . . . it's a whole new world. It brings with it, however, easier ways to communicate than having to meet face-to-face. Many evaluators, therapists, and attorneys will recommend that you communicate only by e-mail with your difficult ex-spouse. This allows for a written record of what is said and also gives you ample time to think through your responses rather than be reactive. Sometimes, your attorney will even help you with this kind of correspondence if there is ongoing court warfare. But, be careful.

This is where you will also use your boundary setting and your assertiveness. Correspond like a sane person and do not engage in battle. You can do it! If you struggle with certain responses, run your e-mail message by your attorney or your friends before sending it.

Your ex may choose to be irresponsible and engage in "digital abuse." For example, your ex may send e-mails or texts harassing you or write nasty, disparaging comments all over Facebook. Your ex may stalk you through the entire territory of social media. Print out and keep copies, forever, of all your ex's messages to you and about you. Unfortunately you may need them even ten years down the road. Some narcissists never give up. One man's ex-wife sued him for their daughter's bat mitzvah money twelve years after the event, even though she had refused to attend the ceremony or reception.

Many vengeful narcissists who feel abandoned lash out on social media. Discuss this abuse with your attorney. You may be better off disengaging from social media until the divorce is settled just to avoid the hassles. You may also take many preventive actions on social media to block your ex from access.

All major social media—Facebook, LinkedIn, Instagram, Twitter, chat apps, and even e-mail programs such as Gmail—offer the ability to block anyone whom you choose. Each method of blocking is slightly different, so consult the specific social media site for instructions for how to do this. The site may also allow you to report abusive behavior to the administrators of the site, who may cancel this person's account. Blocking cuts off contact, but it does not prevent your ex from continuing to say slanderous things about you to his or her followers and friends. If you know that this kind of abuse is going on, your only other remedy is to sue him or her for slander or to get a restraining order preventing this conduct.

Even if you have blocked your ex on social media, you will still have to remain in contact about the children's activities and plans for vacations and visits.

A shared Web calendar where the children's events and activities can be recorded in a single place can be particularly helpful. This can cut down on having to constantly communicate on e-mail about what the children are doing. Find a calendar that tracks who logs in and when and only allows the person who put something on it to remove that event. Many sites also allow you to load documents, such as report cards, that need to be shared with the other parent. Two such sites I am aware of are ShareKids calendar and Our Family Wizard.

Disarming the Narcissist

Disarming someone who likes to shoot is difficult, but the further you get along in your recovery, in your life apart from your ex, and in your happiness, the less likely it is that the narcissist can get to you or trigger you. You will want to get to an emotional place where you have complete neutrality in your feelings for your ex, a place where you then can merely roll your eyes and say, "That's my ex." This takes work and conscious effort, and we are going to discuss further how to do this in the next chapter.

At times you may be caught off guard. When this happens, it is helpful to have a standard phrase you can use to give yourself time to not be reactive. I like using the word *interesting*. For example, your ex throws something at you that shocks or surprises you, and you do not know how to react. You want to scream, but you simply say, "Interesting, I will think about that." Or you just say the word *interesting*. It seems to throw narcissists because they have not gotten to you and they have no idea what you mean. You give them no more. When narcissists are bullies, the best thing to do is to walk away and not engage in their games. Eventually they find someone else to bully. In the end you are laying down your guns but keeping your armor of healing around you.

Your goal is to protect yourself and your children. Working from your own value system, being kind, assertive, and using the coping skills in this chapter along with your internal recovery work, will serve you best.

Where Do We Go from Here?

You must be clear about what is in your power to do and what is not. Your narcissistic ex will likely hold on to his or her injury and keep fighting. You need to take appropriate measures to defend yourself. The key to your recovery, and that of your children, lies in discovering or rediscovering yourself, returning to the core of your being.

Let's move on to recovery. In the next chapter, you will learn specific tools and skills to rebuild and strengthen your authentic self.

CHAPTER EIGHT

MOVING ON: THE ARMOR OF HEALING

Frank Sinatra is commonly credited with saying, "The best revenge is massive success."[1] I agree with that sentiment. When you have been harmed by a relationship with a narcissist, the best revenge is to reclaim your sense of self and life. It is time to take the healing inside.

How deep is your hurt? It depends on a lot of things that are unique to you, such as your family background, how strong you were when you entered the relationship, how long the relationship was, and how bad it was. You have likely suffered damaged self-esteem and a lack of belief in yourself. Many adults I have treated who have had intimate connections with narcissists have been diagnosed with post-traumatic stress disorder caused by extreme verbal, emotional, and psychological abuse. Some have experienced sexual and physical abuse as well.

Some people in your life will not understand the pain or damage that you have suffered. The narcissist presents well to the outside world. If someone doesn't understand your reality, don't look to him or her for sympathy or advice. Listen instead to your gut. Honor your feelings. Work a recovery program so that you are able to move forward in a successful manner for your life and that of your children.

Some people say things like "Get over it already!" or "The past is the past." I hear this a lot from clients whose friends and family want them to forget it and move on. You are not going to stay a victim forever. Your ultimate goal is to move on, but you can't do that without first working at recovery. You cannot leave your emotional baggage unattended. If you don't process your feelings, they will weigh you down and encumber your new life.

Anthony, a client with great insights, told me, "I just got out of a horrible marriage and divorce with a woman who dragged me through the mud for years in terms of self-esteem, court battles, finance wars, custody issues . . . It really took a bite out of me. It feels like I have to be refurbished like a wrecked car. But my sisters and parents keep saying to me that I am living in the past and need to be strong and just get over it. It's not that easy."

Anthony is right. You need to address the trauma and the feelings you've experienced or they will continue to come up and haunt you in years and relationships to come. This chapter will give you a road map to healing.

What Does Recovery Look Like?

In my thirty-plus years working as a therapist and treating children of narcissistic parents, I have developed a recovery model to help you. In my first book, *Will I Ever Be Good Enough? Healing the Daughters of Narcissistic Mothers*, I explained how this model works for adult daughters of narcissistic mothers. In this book, I have adapted the recovery model for people who have been married to or are in a partnership with a narcissist. Let's begin.

Five-Step Recovery Model

Step One	•	Acceptance and Grief
Step Two	•	Psychological Separation
Step Three	•	Becoming Your Authentic Self
Step Four	•	Dealing with Your Ex in Recovery
Step Five	•	Ending the Legacy of Distorted Love

Step One: Acceptance and Grief

To begin your healing, the first step is to accept that your partner has a disorder that cannot change. Remember the Serenity Prayer? Our only hope of change is within ourselves so that we do not pass on to our children the legacy of distorted love. We cannot grieve until we accept the situation as it is.

Acceptance can be difficult. It is tempting to believe that, if we just love enough, do enough, be enough, our actions will change the other person and cure the ills of the relationship. Acceptance means you have to give up the belief and the expectation that your ex will change. You have to accept your ex for who he or she is and no longer expect him or her to meet your needs. You have let go of unrealistic hopes, too. Letting go will free you to focus on your own healing.

You will want to be careful that you don't fall back into familiar ways of thinking. While my client Jackie was working recovery, she realized, "In my family of origin, I was the fixer. I was always trying to make things better for everyone. I was sensitive and kind and listened to them all, but it never really worked. Basically, I grew up being trained as a codependent. It took me a long time to realize that I can't fix anyone but myself. My codependency was even kind of controlling at times. I thought I had let go of this behavior, but with my ex-husband, I kept thinking maybe he will get it. Maybe he will realize what he is missing and start to change or at least be nice again. Maybe I was wrong about him. Maybe he will get over the divorce and we can actually be friends. I actually had dreams that he would suddenly change and all would be good. This really set me up for more disappointment, pain, anger, and angst. I would be excited when he called or kind of looking forward to seeing him at a kid drop-off, and then the other shoe always dropped. I learned the hard way that my being nice and trying to help him just worked against me most of the time. He used it to manipulate me and then was angry at me. It was very confusing until I learned to let go!"

HOW DO I KNOW WHEN I HAVE TOTALLY
ACCEPTED THIS DISORDER IN MY EX?

From time to time you can ask yourself these important questions:

1. Do I continue to wish and hope that my ex will be different each time I talk to him or her?
2. Do I continue to have expectations of him or her?
3. Have I accepted my ex for who he or she is and do not expect it to change?
4. Do I feel any sense of entitlement about my own needs with my ex?
5. Do I now rely on myself to meet most of my needs?
6. Have I let go?

Only after you have let go of these expectations and desires will you be able to grieve the loss of the relationship. You are no longer taking things personally, you have built up your internal defenses using strategies from the prior chapter to deal in the present, and you are now ready to heal.

Before we move on, let me clarify something about grief. You've probably heard about the five stages of grief. These were described by Dr. Elisabeth Kübler-Ross in her pioneering work *On Death and Dying*. Dr. Kübler-Ross lists the stages as denial, anger, bargaining, depression, and then acceptance.[2]

If you are familiar with the stages of grief, you may wonder if my five-step model overlaps. Yes, it does. The five stages of grief as described by Dr. Kübler-Ross are all included in the first stage of the recovery model described here. But you will notice that in my model, acceptance comes first. It is the emerging from denial. As explained above, acceptance of the disorder of narcissism is needed before the grief work is effective.

GRIEF

When we lose someone or something, we grieve. When we divorce, many aspects of our lives are uprooted and changed. We let go of the past and work through feelings associated with these changes. We let go of the old and slowly make room for the new.

If you are an adult child of narcissistic parents, you will find grieving to be even more complicated. In divorce you will simultaneously be processing the loss of your wishes for a good parent as well as your hope for a good partner. You will likely do grief work that you have not done in the past. Some of my clients describing a current relationship find themselves veering off to discuss the same traits exhibited by their family members.

Annie was telling me about her custody battles with her ex when she suddenly said, "Dealing with Brian was just like dealing with my mother. It made me realize I married my mother! Was I this attracted to the familiar? Brian and my mother were both manipulative. They used sugary, fake kindness to try to get their way, but if I resisted, it would turn into narcissistic rage. Neither was able to see me as I am with my own thoughts and feelings. It made me realize that I had to do double recovery."

Thomas came to therapy to address his high-conflict divorce but found that in almost every session he was talking about his narcissistic father. He told me, "It is the control I felt from my dad. He tried to control everything about me and my life. If I disagreed, he would get angry. I think I learned to be afraid of anger and conflict, so when I got married, I tried hard to avoid conflict with my wife, too. It made it difficult for me to set boundaries and stand my ground on anything, and eventually my wife just ran the show and lost respect for me. I felt small with her just like I did with my dad."

Once you can discern your grief over your disappointed expectations, you can start letting go of the past and make room in your mind and emotions for better feelings and expectations.

NARCISSISTIC FAMILY WOUNDS

If while reading this book you realize that you come from a family where one or both of your parents are also narcissistic, your recovery program will be more intense and complicated. You will need to go through acceptance and grief with your family, too.

When my client Heather was in her early thirties, her narcissistic mother sent her a picture of a mother smiling and looking pretty in a hospital bed. On the back of the photo the mother wrote: "Heather—This is your mom the day you were born. I know I have a picture of you that we took in the hospital, but I can't find it." Although Heather was named after her grandmother, her mother often called her Missy because Heather was a "mistake," an unplanned pregnancy. In fact, Heather's mother even introduced her to others saying, "This is Missy, you know, our little mistake!" Her mother told her she was afraid to tell anyone when she got pregnant with Heather because others might think she was a dirty old lady. Heather once asked her mother, "Why didn't you have an abortion?" The hurt in Heather's eyes when she told me this story was visible. She had internalized messages from her unhappy childhood such as "I am invisible," "I am not as important as Mom," "I was an unwanted child," "I am unworthy."

You can see how the messages were clearly a result of her mother's narcissism, and if you wonder about your own upbringing or if you had narcissistic parents, take the following survey, which is adapted from my prior book, *Will I Ever Be Good Enough? Healing the Daughters of Narcissistic Mothers*. The same questions apply if you had a narcissistic father.

IS THIS MY PARENT?

Narcissism is a spectrum disorder with the most severe end of the spectrum considered a narcissistic personality disorder. A parent can have several narcissistic traits and not fit the personality disorder but even with a few traits can negatively affect his children in insidious ways. You will see many similarities here to the checklist on a narcissistic love partner.

Check or circle all those that apply to your relationship with your mother or father.

1. When you discuss your life issues with your parent, does he or she divert the discussion to talk about himself or herself?
2. When you discuss your feelings with your parent, does he or she try to top the feeling with his or her own?
3. Does your parent act jealous of you?
4. Does your parent lack empathy for your feelings?
5. Does your parent only support those things you do that reflect on him or her as a "good parent"?
6. Have you consistently felt a lack of emotional closeness with your parent?
7. Have you consistently questioned whether your parent likes you or loves you?
8. Does your parent only do things for you when others can see?
9. When something happens in your life (accident, illness, divorce), does your parent react with how it will affect him or her rather than how you feel?
10. Is or was your parent overly conscious of what others think (neighbors, friends, family, coworkers)?
11. Does your parent deny his or her own feelings?
12. Does your parent blame things on you or others rather than take responsibility for his or her own feelings or actions?
13. Is your parent hurt easily and then carries a grudge for a long time without resolving the problem?
14. Do you feel that you were a slave to your parent?
15. Do you feel responsible for your parent's ailments (headaches, stress, and illness)?
16. Did you have to take care of your parent's physical needs as a child?
17. Do you feel unaccepted by your parent?

18. Do you feel your parent was critical of you?
19. Do you feel helpless in the presence of your parent?
20. Are you shamed often by your parent?
21. Do you feel your parent knows the real you?
22. Does your parent act as if the world should revolve around him or her?
23. Do you find it difficult to be a separate person from your parent?
24. Does your parent appear phony to you?
25. Does your parent want to control your choices?
26. Does your parent swing from egotistical to depressed mood?
27. Did you feel you had to take care of your parent's emotional needs as a child?
28. Do you feel manipulated in the presence of your parent?
29. Do you feel valued by your parent for what you do rather than who you are?
30. Is your parent controlling, acting like a victim or martyr?
31. Does your parent make you act different from how you really feel?
32. Does your parent compete with you?
33. Does your parent always have to have things his or her way?[3]

All of these questions relate to narcissistic traits. The more questions you checked, the more likely it is that your parent has narcissistic traits and this has caused some difficulty for you growing up. You may be more vulnerable to choosing friends or love relationships with narcissistic people. Your child will be dealing with these traits in his or her narcissistic parent.

GRIEF AND TRAUMA WORK

The next part of Step One is trauma resolution. This is the most important and most difficult element of recovery. You may have learned to deny, stuff, or not deal with feelings in order to survive in the narcissistic relationship. Now it is time to bring those feelings to the surface and process them. Processing feelings is different from just telling your story. It is experiencing these feelings, perhaps for the first time, until they are neutralized. Many people want to skip this important part because it hurts, but it is worth taking the time to really do this work. It is difficult and painful, but it's better to go through this now than to wait and carry these feelings around with you any longer. You want to be free of all this, but if you skip this step, those feelings will keep coming up.

Let me give you an example of the difference between telling your story and processing feelings. I could tell you about going to my beloved grandmother's funeral. I could include many details, such as information about my relationship with her, traveling to the funeral, seeing family members, flowers, traditions, and funeral-service details, even how she was presented and celebrated. My account could be factual and even interesting, but devoid of feeling. This is very different from telling you about going to the funeral and describing as well as experiencing my feelings of sorrow or happiness in seeing other family members, of remembering our times with my grandmother, of the joy and connection we felt in reliving our memories of life with her.

To process a loss, we must reexperience the feelings until the pain is worked through, *not* simply remembered. The more feelings you embrace and discuss, the more desensitized you become to the sting of them. This does not mean you will never feel them again, but it dissipates their strength so that powerful waves of emotion do not keep getting in the way of your daily functioning. If you do not do this, these emotions keep coming up either in your thoughts or your behavior patterns.

Because many people have never done structured grief work, I am going to give you some exercises that you can use, as follows:

1. *Journaling.* Journaling has many benefits. Find a journal that you like to write in and take time each day to write down your feelings. Don't worry how you say things, just focus on getting those

feelings down on paper. Some people do better with this on the computer and make a daily journal document. Others like to write by hand. Find what works best for you. It will be cathartic.

Some clients resist journaling because they fear that someone might read their diary. Some have had the awful experience as a child of a parent reading their personal feelings and being shamed for them or getting in trouble for writing down truths that make others uncomfortable. I understand, but remember, you can burn or destroy your journal after you have dealt with feelings. You may even want to make a ceremony of burning or throwing out your journal to purge yourself of these old feelings.

Sally resisted writing a journal, saying, "I'm a writer. I am always sitting at the computer or taking notes on something. It just seemed so hard for me to also make time to journal. But, when I made myself do it, I found it to be very cathartic and helpful, and it was actually very different from my work. Plus, the journaling I did with no judgment on how it sounds or how I write. I just blurt out what is going on and it feels good. Some days, I just write feelings that I am in touch with that day. It did help me a lot."

2. *Sit with the pain.* Allow yourself to sit for fifteen to thirty minutes at a time and just feel. If you can tolerate longer, do it. I know this is hard to do. We all have busy lives and are on the go, but to allow feelings to surface, you may need some structured quiet time. When the feelings come up, don't run from them, but instead sit with them. They won't kill you, they will just be there. Breathe through them, write about them, and let them be. Learning to do this is important, as many of us like to numb or swish away any bad feelings as soon as they hit our awareness. If you take the time to do this several times per week, you will find those feelings get processed more quickly. Some people do this as a part of their meditation exercises.

Mark was resistant to sitting still and feeling old emotions, but found this ultimately helpful. He said, "I did not think there was any way I could do this. We have two toddlers in the house and noisy teenagers—there are toys everywhere—and I have a million things to do. If I sat still, I would be making lists in my head of everything I have to do and get more anxious. I am a 'doing' kind of guy and have to be moving. But, I tried it, late at night when the house settled down, and surprisingly, with a flood of feelings I started to cry. I did not realize how I had stuffed so many feelings from that prior relationship. I know this will help me get through all this now. I can't say I love it, but in the long run, it will really help me get more in touch with me."

3. *Reflect on the pain and disappointments of this relationship.* To do this, you can write a letter to yourself or to an imaginary person, explaining your pain and disappointment. Talk about what went wrong, how you were hurt, why you could not stay, how you lost yourself and your belief in you. In this reflection, expect your sadness, anger, rage, shame, guilt, and disappointments all to come to the surface so you can examine them and feel them.

Paula found a creative way to do this. She said, "I decided to write to my mini-me. I would write letters to the child within me, whom I called Mini. I asked her how she was feeling and let her talk about her deep feelings being in this sucky relationship. It was easier to let her off the hook because I visualized her as mini, and I did not blame her so much for staying so long! Mini and I have had some great conversations. For some reason, this is helping me to quit stuffing. I'm also liking my little Mini, and that helps, too! I can be empathetic with her."

4. *Write about your ideal love relationship.* This exercise can give you hope and help you figure out what you want and deserve. What would the ideal relationship look like for you? What would your partner be like on the *inside*? If you start going down the path of "it will never happen for me," remind yourself that you will need time to recover first, and then, yes, it can happen for you. Most people post-divorce say they will never get involved with anyone again. But

they often feel different when they've completed this divorce adjustment and trauma work.

Ken learned a lot from this exercise and reflected, "Hmmm, this was really cool in the beginning, dreaming of that perfect woman for me, but as I really looked at what I was writing, some lightbulbs went off. I was totally focusing on beauty and sex and all the wrong things, and not one word about what kind of lovely and kind person she would be. I also saw some of my own narcissistic traits in that there was a lot in my writing about what she would be doing for *me*! Yikes! That scared me. I started to turn this around and feel so much better about what I really want and need in a connection with a woman. I think it will help me with dating when I am ready. I am that typical guy who used to look for beauty and sex, ya know? God, we do learn the hard way!"

5. *Reflect on the parts of you that were lost in this relationship.* When you are involved with narcissists, you lose a part of yourself because you are so busy catering to them. It is time-consuming to feed their endless narcissistic needs. You may have let go of hobbies or activities that you enjoyed or music that you loved. What parts of your creative self did you lose to the narcissistic relationship and its many demands?

Stacy told me, "I was so trained to take care of others that I became a therapist just like my mom. It was my role in the family to take care of everyone. When I got married, I fell right into the role of caretaking my narcissistic husband until I became utterly exhausted. Now that I am divorced, I am able for the first time in my life to think about myself and who I am. I just joined a rock band and am expanding my music talent. Wow, this is fun! I am finding so many creative sides of me that were not expressed before. I was the classic codependent. It's sad to me that I had lost so much of myself over the years, but I am catching up now. I'm loving it!"

6. *Eye movement desensitization reprocessing.* As a therapist, I am a fan of eye movement desensitization reprocessing (EMDR). This trauma treatment uses a rapid-eye-movement technique. It helps you get

to, process, and desensitize deeply buried feelings, all at the same time. EMDR is effective but needs to be done with a trained therapist.

When I first heard how EMDR works, I was skeptical of it, but this technique has proved helpful in treating combat veterans with PTSD. I use it almost weekly in therapy sessions with my clients for a variety of trauma issues. You can investigate more about this technique at the international EMDR website, emdria.org. You can also use this site to find EMDR-trained therapists in your area.

7. *Psychotherapy.* I do advise you to find an experienced therapist to assist you with your grief and trauma work. Even though you can do these exercises on your own, it is helpful to find a therapist who understands the debilitating effects of narcissism and is willing to guide you through the five-step recovery model.

8. *Watching movies.* Some clients' feelings are so buried they seem unreachable. Sometimes, watching movies can trigger the emotions to which these people need access. I have a list of movies in the " 'Reel' Therapy" section at the end of this book. If you feel emotionally numb, movies may help you let yourself feel grief and other emotions again.

Step Two: Psychological Separation

As people mature, each must separate from his or her family of origin to become fully grown-up and a separate individual. Psychological literature describes this process of separation/individuation as differentiation. This internal process has nothing to do with geographical separation. After you accomplish this part of your development, you are able to step outside family dynamics rather than being pulled into emotional reactivity. As you separate, you outgrow your role in your family of origin and become your authentic self.

If you were raised by a narcissistic parent or come from a narcissistic family, you may not have been able to accomplish this healthy separation/individuation due to the stifling enmeshment with or neglect by narcissistic parents. Some narcissistic parents engulf and ignore, switching back and forth between these two extremes. You may also still carry the internalized messages from this upbringing that say you are not good enough or not worthy of love.

The same dynamic holds true when in an intimate relationship with a narcissist. You get pulled into his or her web and into a distorted reality and lose your solid sense of self. It reminds me of a book published in 1997 by Jordan and Margaret Paul titled *Do I Have to Give Up Me to Be Loved by You?* You can internalize negative messages that you will now have to release to find your own reality. Let's look at how this works:

Your narcissistic ex used to tell you . . .	Now you journal . . .
You are lazy and dumb.	The things you do that are productive and the things you have accomplished in your life that took your intelligence.
You are not attractive.	The things you like about your appearance. Review compliments others have given you over the years.
No one else will ever love you.	To remind yourself that this world has many people and a match is out there for you when you are ready.
You are not good enough.	The things you do well and the personal qualities that you are proud of, such as your character, value system, and integrity.
Your feelings are wrong.	That you feel what you feel and have that right. You remember that feelings don't have brains. You are learning to trust your feelings again.

These are just a few examples of the kinds of internalized messages we can come away with when separating from or divorcing a narcissist. Work this exercise for the specific negative messages that your ex has given you.

In this step you are leaving your partner's distorted world and coming back to your own reality, redefining yourself as outside of this relationship. Reclaiming you. Only *you* get to define you. If you want feedback from others, choose those whom you can trust to give you honest and fair feedback that is in your best interests. In short, don't go to a narcissist to define you. You will walk away carrying their projections of their self-loathing.

Stephanie described how she became more aware of herself after the divorce. She said, "My ex-husband, Ben, constantly told me I was not good enough. It didn't really matter what it was. I was too fat, I didn't keep the house clean, I didn't get the laundry done on time, I spent too much on groceries, I didn't feed the kids right. I could go on and on. After the divorce, I began therapy and worked on my self-esteem. I started talking back to those negative messages. When I began to look at who I am and not what I do, things began to change for me. Ben was about 'doing' and not 'being.' I got pulled into that. Now I give myself credit. I am now making lists of what a great mom I am, how I can tune in to my kids, and how I have done a good job raising them. I have good friends who love me. Although this is ongoing work, I am beginning to see me now and I like me."

Step Three: Becoming Your Authentic Self

Now that you have cleaned up trauma and worked on grief and separation, you are ready to build your authentic self. You likely got crushed in your previous relationship and need rebuilding, polishing, or perhaps some tune-up. You may even feel that you are mining for your authentic self now. You may be asking, "Who am I really?" You may also be saying, "I have no idea how to do this." Here are some exercises to help in the mining and refining. You are in there somewhere, I promise!

1. *The "I Am" list*. You can start with making an "I Am" list. You start with a clean piece of paper and start each sentence with *I am* and then finish the sentence. Start with the clear, simple, obvious ones, and let your brain and emotions take you to the deeper you. For example: *I am a woman. I am a man. I am a mother. I am a father. I am forty-six years old. I am a resident of Chicago. I am a graphic designer*. Then you allow this to go deeper to the character traits of who you are. Such as: *I am an honest person. I am an empathetic parent. I am true to my word. I am an energetic worker. I am a good person*. Keep going until you exhaust your thoughts and feelings.

I have found this to be helpful for clients in therapy. As they keep going with the list, they begin to get in touch with the things they like about themselves. Even those who struggle and say, "There is nothing to say, I am empty," as they work this, they do find many things about themselves that are like silver and gold. Then we polish the metals!

2. *The collage of you*. Make a collage out of photos that represent the different aspects of who you are. Cut out pictures from magazines or download images from the Internet. Search for photos that reflect your character, show things that are important to you, or capture who you are. Google for images of the characteristics that display the real you. Then make your own piece of art, pasting them together in the collage of *you*!

3. *Your value system*. Make a list of what you value the most in life. What gives your life meaning and significance? What gives you a deep sense of fulfillment?

4. *Your interests*. What are your unique interests in life? Make a list of them.

5. *Talents*. We each have unique talents. Write out yours, even if you have not used them in some time. You may be naturally artistic, musical, or athletic. It may be time for you to pursue your talent in a career or a hobby and allow your creative side to operate in the world.

6. *Passions*. Passion can be different from talent, although sometimes they are the same. A passion is something you are deeply interested in or want to learn more about. List yours.

7. *Health*. I often find that clients in early recovery have neglected their health in many ways while in a stressful relationship. Taking good care of your body supports your mental health. Do you need a physical, a dental appointment, a mammogram, or other medical checkups? Do you have a medical need you have ignored or neglected? Are you eating well and getting the proper rest and exercise? This is the time to nurture your physical health.

I hope you are closer to finding your authentic self. This can be an ongoing journey so keep it up. The closer you get to you, the closer you get to the success that Frank Sinatra talked about: "The best revenge is massive success!" I am not talking about what you do, but about who you are. You do not need to make a million dollars, but you want to feel like a million.

Step Four: Dealing with Your Ex in Recovery

Now that you have accepted the disorder in your ex-spouse and worked through the trauma, you are rebuilding your authentic self. You have shifted on the inside. You can feel it. You will begin to act differently with your ex. In the past, you could get triggered easily and collapse. You may have internalized messages, blamed yourself, tried to fix things, or just felt bad.

Now you are more whole and grounded. You don't topple over as easily. Your defenses are strong, and you are not as vulnerable to manipulation. You are empowered by setting firm boundaries and communicating clearly.

In this step, you practice staying in your authentic self and not reacting. Stay clear about what you need and what is right for the children. You don't let yourself feel the false guilt that your ex tries to trigger. Validate your feelings and work on trusting yourself.

In the past, Karen was easily triggered when her ex-husband put her down. She shared this recently as she was working on this step: "I just came back from a parent-teacher conference for my son, and my ex was there. He usually brags to the teacher about himself and is not that into the child. He also has an unbelievable way of always saying something that puts me down as a parent. This time was no different. The teacher was suggesting that our son become involved in some sports or outside activities to help his social skills. Sure enough, my ex had to bring up money, child support, the cost of the divorce, and tried to make it sound like it was my fault that we could not afford anything extra for our son. I calmly let him finish and then smiled and thanked the teacher for her great suggestion. I told her I would love to work with her on this for our son. It was so different for me than the past, where I would have gone home and cried for three days about how awful he is. This time, I rolled my eyes and just did my own thing as a parent and it felt great."

Intently listening to your intuition is an important part of this step. Deep down you can feel things and your body will give you signs if you listen. We make mistakes when we don't listen to this inner voice. Pay attention to any red flags your intuition sends up.

John was used to being manipulated by his ex-wife. It took him a long time to understand and listen to his feelings so he could set boundaries with her. With time, he became more aware of the warning signals going off in his head. He said wryly, "That girl could ring my bell! She was so manipulative and she usually did it with her feminine ways or baby neediness that really got me. It was like I knew it, but I couldn't stop reacting to it because I felt guilty if I didn't respond like she wanted. But I learned how to turn the ringer off! It's freedom really. And now instead of hearing her emergencies, I listen to my own intuition and that guides me in the right direction."

Step Four requires a lot of attention and practice. You allow the internal shift to continue, so you are operating in a different manner with your ex. If you find you still get triggered or continue to have collapses, go back and do more grief and trauma work from the previous steps. When you get triggered, it just means that you have not cleaned up the trauma, and that's okay. It can take a while. This is a journey.

Step Five: Ending the Legacy of Distorted Love

Step Five is about ending the legacy of distorted love in your life. Doing this step helps shape a brighter future and is an ongoing part of your recovery. We will look at Step Five from the perspective of your relationships with yourself, friends, family, future love relationships, and your children.

BE COMFORTABLE ON YOUR OWN

To do the recovery work and develop a peaceful relationship with yourself, first it is important to be on your own for a while before jumping into another relationship. While it is tempting to get back into the dating scene, give yourself some time. If you have never been alone, you'll find spending time with yourself is worth it. You need to be your significant other for a while. If you are lonely, seek comfort from friends and family, join support groups, or find community in activities that interest you. Dating sites will not make it all better. If you take the old you into another relationship, you will be at risk of repeating the same damaging pattern.

Jerry admits he had never been alone in his life. He went straight from his parents' home to living with his girlfriend, whom he later married. "When we divorced, I felt like a kid lost in the woods! Not only did I feel this weird loneliness, but I did not know how to be with myself. I was so used to orbiting around my ex-wife and doing what she wanted, I never had time to think about what I wanted. I did the same thing growing up with what I now understand was my own narcissistic mother. The temptation to jump on dating sites—jeez, what a candy store—was calling me big-time. I knew better, but I couldn't resist when a lovely woman responded to me and wanted to go out. My therapist had warned me to keep it to casual dating so I thought this was okay to try. But, before I knew it, I was involved again in a rather serious way and realized I had not taken the time for recovery or to even find myself. And, I know this is to be expected, I soon began to see some narcissistic traits in this new woman. I had repeated the pattern and couldn't even believe it after all I had been through. I now see that I have to make myself do this alone thing. It's hard, but I am doing it and finding it very helpful."

NEW LOVE RELATIONSHIPS

You may wonder when is the right time to allow yourself to start dating. The answer is simply this: when you have dealt with being dependent or codependent. Let me explain.

If you were dependent: You were relying on your ex for most everything and allowed him or her to make decisions for you. Your dependence may have been financial or just that your ex took the lead. You had to follow, or it caused fights and conflict.

If you were codependent: you were taking care of others to the exclusion of taking care of yourself.

Your goal now is to work toward an interdependent relationship. This is when you and your partner have a balance of give-and-take. You have reciprocity. Some days you may be the caretaker, and other days it is the role of your partner. It bounces back and forth between you in a balanced way. You are able to lean on each other.

INTERDEPENDENT HEALTHY RELATIONSHIPS

When you start to date someone, go back to chapter 2 and revisit the checklist for a healthy relationship. In the first stages of relationships La-La Land can be deceiving. Give any new relationship the time you need to sort out who the real person is and what real issues come with him or her. Everyone has an exception to this rule and has at least one story to tell about a friend or acquaintance who met and married quickly and is still happily together with that spouse. But this is not the norm. Second marriages have a higher divorce rate than first marriages. I would advise you to stay on the alert. Be wary of getting involved in another unhealthy relationship. If you did it once, you could be vulnerable to doing it again.

When you start dating someone new, remember the two best questions to ask yourself: "Does this person bring out the best in me?" and "How do I feel in the presence of this person?" You are focusing on how you feel, not if the person likes you and what you might do to "make" the person like you, as you had to do with your ex.

This is also a good time to reflect on self-blame and self-doubt. Do you feel less of both? Are you trusting your gut reactions and intuition? Are you believing in yourself and your own feelings?

Check your friends and community. Now that you are attuned to what narcissism is, you may find that you have also gathered a flock of narcissists as friends, and it may be time to fly the coop. You may need a cleaning-out period and time to search for new, more meaningful relationships. To determine this, ask yourself about reciprocity with your friends. You can do the same checklist as we did for love relationships. Can you set boundaries with your friends that they respect? Are your friends competitive? Do they have trouble celebrating the real you? Can your friends bond with you and be empathetic but also celebrate your successes? You want to gather people in your life who add to your life and don't drain you of your emotional energy.

Letting go can be a difficult, sad process. Don't do this too quickly or before you have done your own grief work. But if toxic folks are in the way of your recovery, it is okay to let them go.

YOUR CHILDREN

Once you have your own recovery in progress, you will be able to better help your children cope with your narcissistic ex. While you can divorce this person, your child or children cannot. You can do much to give your child or children what they need. You can teach them about real love.

This parenting journey carries much responsibility; I have dedicated the next chapter to helping you with your wounded children.

CHAPTER NINE

EMPATHETIC PARENTING: YOUR WOUNDED CHILD

As a loving parent, you have "double duty." The antithesis of narcissism is empathy, meaning empathetic parenting is the way to try to heal and to protect your children. Your task is to counter the effects of your ex-spouse's narcissistic behavior. You will treasure the moments when your children are in your care, because this is your opportunity to allow them to feel safe and secure. As I said before, parenting is more than providing a roof over the head, clothes to wear, and food to eat. Fortunately, all the work that you have done in recovery will help you to be the parent your children need.

It is painful to realize that even though you were able to choose to leave this dysfunctional marriage, your children will always have a narcissistic parent. Your ex does not have the ability to tune in to your child's hopes, dreams, joys, fears, or pain.

Susan said sadly, "I love my daughter so much. I can't regret a marriage that produced this beautiful little girl, but it hurts me profoundly when I cannot protect her from the constant harm of her narcissistic father."

I could hear the frustration in his voice as Geoff told me, "During the custody battle, I swear my ex's biggest concern was that she did not want to look bad. More than that, she wanted to look good. She had no problem when the girls were diagnosed with attention deficit disorder and prescribed ADD medication. That diagnosis did not reflect badly on her. But it was a whole different story when I wanted to have them evaluated by a psychiatrist because they were experiencing anxiety and depression. She would have nothing to do with this. I think she felt it reflected badly on her. It was so hard to get help for my daughters! It felt like I was beating my head against a wall, not to mention the money I had to spend to get the court to order this evaluation. She wouldn't concede anything unless it was on her terms. The kids are the ones who really lose, and it breaks my heart for them."

Remember that in your own recovery, you had to accept your ex's disorder as it affected you. Now you have to understand and accept your ex's parenting limitations. Accepting those limitations means that you don't expect or hope that your coparent will change. Instead, focus on your own parenting behavior.

What Is Empathetic Parenting?

Empathetic parenting will allow you to be a great parent and to fight the good fight against your ex's narcissism. As an empathetic parent you tune in to your child's emotional world and parent from this viewpoint at all times. In every situation that has any kind of emotional weight, the first thing that you do is understand, acknowledge, and validate your child's feelings. You do that before you move to any other actions. When you develop that habit, your child will not only feel heard, seen, and known, but will also learn to recognize the landscape of the emotional world and find his or her way through it.

This does not mean that your child always gets his or her way, or that you allow your child to manipulate you. It means that you take the time to understand what is up with your babe before you react to him or her. When you take that time, you are better able to help your child learn how to acknowledge their feelings while also managing their behavior. This is what we all want in our intimate relationships. Why not teach your child loving interaction from the get-go?

When a child feels heard, it's easier to work with his or her wants, desires, and needs. If children feel that you respect them, they are more likely to treat your boundaries and rules respectfully, too. You are teaching them a skill that will assist them in their future relationships as well as when they have children. I teach about empathy every day; it is the basis and core of my work. In this difficult world, I believe that empathy could make a positive difference everywhere. Let me tell you why.

I have been a practicing psychotherapist for more than thirty years. During that time, I have worked with thousands of clients, ranging in age from three to eighty-three. When clients first come to me, I find they want to be heard and understood, more than anything else, no matter their age or situation. This is the foundation on which the client and I can build a therapeutic and trusting alliance.

However, when people ask for a therapist's help, their goal is not simply to have someone else understand them. Their greater need is to understand themselves. They need this self-understanding to deal with the issues that brought them to therapy. I work with clients to help them acknowledge and validate their feelings. We work with feelings before trying to solve problems. We solve problems by processing feelings.

When children have parents who are not attuned to their emotional world, they find it difficult to learn to trust their own feelings. If they cannot trust their feelings, they grow up with crippling self-doubt. The historical and primary concern of many adult children of narcissistic parents is that they were not seen, heard, or understood in their childhood.

An adult client who was in therapy for child sexual abuse perpetrated by his father told me several years ago, "Even though the horror of the sex abuse has been a difficult issue to come to terms with, I have to say that growing up in a narcissistic family was at least as damaging as the sexual abuse. It has affected me every day of my life. The narcissism was the killer for me. I was always defined by whether or not I fit their conscripted mold and was not taught to define or even know myself."

Our culture is becoming more narcissistic, focusing on image and wealth, valuing people for what they do rather than who they are. When children are also valued for what they do rather than for who they are, we create a generation who do not know how to build worthwhile lives and quality relationships. Instead, we should be helping them to build their lives on a strong foundation of self-understanding, so that they can become capable, caring, and good people.

Practice Being an Empathetic Parent

Relating to our children with empathy means first understanding what they are feeling. They may express their feelings through behavior, words, or both. You start with a simple reflection of "This is what I am hearing you say" or "It seems like you are feeling angry, let's talk about what you are angry about." When we don't do this, we are at risk of making assumptions that are not true, or projecting our own feelings onto the child.

Let's look at some examples:

Your little girl is upset because she did not get what she wanted: a toy, a candy, a cookie, something important to her. She reacts by saying, "I hate you!" If you come right back with your gut response, it might be an angry statement like "Don't you dare talk to me like that!" or an immediate punishment such as "Go to your room now!" The gut response leaves your daughter feeling unheard and usually makes the situation worse. Instead, try responding to the feeling first. For instance, you might say, "I know you don't hate me, sweetheart, but it sure looks like you are mad." You should also validate the feeling, as in "I know it makes you mad that you can't have it and I understand. Sometimes I get mad, too, when I can't have something I want, but let's just talk about it." This takes time and energy but is worth it. When she knows that she is heard, usually she will settle down. That's when you can explain the boundaries and the rules but also let her know it is okay to have this feeling. Parenting with empathy takes more time, but it allows you to take the conversation to a better place.

Your fifth grader is upset that he cannot spend the night at his friend's. He reacts by hitting the wall and slamming his door. Again your first response is probably to be angry with your son, and next you believe he needs to be punished. Don't do it. Try helping him to identify the feeling by reflecting it. You might say, "It looks like you are sad and disappointed that this is not working out right now." Then validate: "I understand that feeling and it is not fun to feel disappointed or sad. In fact, it is really hard." "I was feeling sad this week because I could not get off work in time to see your game." "I can see this is hard for you. Let's talk about how we can make this happen at another time."

Your teenager wants to go to the mall, but you can't drive her there right this minute. She throws a fit. She says something dramatic like "You don't even care if I spend time with my friends!" You stifle the zingers that you might want to launch, like "That's true, I don't care this minute, I just need to pay the bills." Instead you say, "Let's talk about what you are really feeling and why." A teenager can tell you more than a young child. Maybe she can identify the feeling of disappointment or even the fear that her friends will not like her anymore if she can't go. You can validate those feelings and talk about how important her feelings are to you. It's important to remember that deeper things are usually going on beneath every conversation. If you respect your daughter's deeper feelings, rather than just looking at her surface wants and desires and perhaps calling her a drama queen, she will feel respected and will in turn respect you more for dealing with her in this way. It will then be much easier to talk with her about finding a better way to handle her next request.

These simple responses done in this sequence (reflect, validate, and empathize) can make all the difference. During the first step, you ignore the context of whatever is going on to focus on the feelings. As an adult, you also just want to be heard and validated. You can have conversations with people who disagree with you, but in the end what you care about is if you are treated with respect. Think about the last time you were upset and how different people responded. Who truly cared about your feelings? Who tried to tell you what to do or solve your problem for you? Sometimes people try to top your story or tell a similar story thinking they are empathizing with you. You just want to be heard. When we are heard, we feel real.

One of my favorite children's books is *The Velveteen Rabbit* by Margery Williams. In this book the rabbit and the Skin Horse talk about love and becoming real. The Skin Horse gives this advice to the rabbit:

> It doesn't happen all at once . . . you become. It takes a long time. That's why it doesn't happen often to people who break easily or have sharp edges, or who have to be carefully kept. Generally, by the time you are Real, most of your hair has been loved off, and your eyes drop out and you get loose in your joints and very shabby. But these things don't matter at all, because once you are Real you can't be ugly, except to people who don't understand.[1]

Simple Tools of Empathetic Parenting

- Identify the feeling.
- Reflect back the feeling.
- Give validation and empathy toward the feeling.
- Ignore the context until these things are done.
- Then deal with the context.

You may think that at times you can't ignore the context as it is a danger to the child or someone else. You are right. In those kinds of situations, you behave differently. First, you stop the dangerous behavior. Then you follow through with the tools of empathetic parenting, starting with reflective listening and validation. In taking this approach, you are *not* giving your children the message that it is okay to hurt either themselves or anyone else. You are just trying to understand what is going on with the children to help them recognize and manage this feeling.

If this parenting approach is new to you, it may not come naturally at first. If you were raised in a narcissistic family, you may find it especially difficult. Keep working on it, because this is what your child needs from you.

How Do I Teach My Child about Feelings?

Five-year-old Jake rushed into my office for his first therapy session and jumped onto the couch. He was charming, red-haired, fiery, and curious. He was told he was meeting his new "feelings doctor." I began to explain what "feelings doctors" did, and he listened with adorable concentration. Then he suddenly blurted out, "I like your office, but there's one thing missing here." I asked him what that was. He said, "Where's the TV?" I explained to him that he was here to talk about his feelings, and if we had a television, that would get in the way of our talking. As I was explaining, Jake gave me this knowing look and said, "Well, that's the point!"

While amused by the precocious candor, I also knew that Jake's parents had brought him in because he was acting out, having tantrums both at home and at school. He refused to listen or take direction. The parents were at their wit's end. While deeply concerned, they were also clueless about the importance of giving their child a voice. Tears and tantrums are red flags. Often children do not know how to process, or even identify, what they are feeling. They can't listen to their parents because they haven't been heard or seen by them. Tantrums are often their honest response to something going on in their lives or how they are unwittingly being treated by sometimes even well-intentioned parents. If they have narcissistic parents, this is a given.

Our culture influences how we value our children's achievements and personal qualities; our culture values accomplishments over character. Lack of accountability, entitlement, and dissociation from self have become the norm, rather than the exception. Feeling invisible and unheard stops healthy emotional development and prevents people from developing a true sense of self. If children are conscripted to fit a mold of what their narcissist parent wants them to be, if they are not allowed to experience and express their authentic selves, they become emotionally stunted and damaged. They remain damaged as adults. So your job as the "double duty" parent is to help your children identify their feelings.

In child therapy we work with the four basic feelings: sad, mad, glad, and scared. You can do the same with your children. If they cannot identify a feeling, you can try to help them give it a name, as long as you don't do it for them. You can also model talking about your own feelings in ways that are appropriate for children. I often recommend that families gather at the end of each day to talk about the events of the day. Instead of asking, "What happened in school today?" you might ask, "What made you guys mad today?" "What made you sad?" "What are you feeling glad about?" "Anybody feeling scared about anything?" Volunteer some of your own feelings to get the conversation started. With practice, children learn to find these feelings in themselves and voice them more easily. I'm a believer in families making it a priority to have a sit-down dinner together, and the family dinner table is a good place to have this kind of conversation.

A fun exercise to help children identify their feelings is to make up stories that have to do with different feelings. One story is about a mad or angry person. One is about a sad person. One is about a scared person. You can, of course, add stories for other feelings. You tell the story, but don't say the feeling. The child must guess what the person in the story might be feeling. You can also use children's books about feelings to discuss different situations and the feelings they bring up.

To help children practice empathy, when you are discussing things as a family, you can have the kids reflect what feeling someone is having. For example, Johnny is telling about someone who called him a name at school today. Megan, his sister, can practice saying something reflective such as "John, I bet you felt very sad when that happened today, because it hurt your feelings."

With young children, you can play the "faces" game. Everyone has to make a face and the family has to guess what the feeling is.

Another game is "feeling guessing" with a movie. You turn off the sound and just watch the faces, and everyone calls out the feeling they are guessing from the expression on the actors' faces.

With young children another tool that can be especially helpful is "feelings charts." These charts have faces depicting many different feelings. If you google *free downloadable feelings charts*, you will probably find something that you like. Print out a feelings chart and put it on your refrigerator so it will be handy when you need some help identifying one of your child's feelings. Even small children can pick the face that most resembles how they feel. Children will expand their feeling word vocabulary as they grow.

How Do I Teach My Child to Manage Feelings?

Once children learn to identify feelings, they also need to learn how to manage them. Feelings have to be processed or they don't go away. You don't want your child to just be quiet and stuff the feelings inside. Repressed feelings can turn into addiction, aggression, depression, and other mental health disorders. Helping your child talk about a feeling is important. You don't have to agree with the feelings, but you do have to acknowledge them.

Here are some strategies to help children manage and process feelings:

- Talk the feelings through while you are validating them.
- If your children are younger, you can have them draw a picture of their feelings and then talk about the drawing.
- Sometimes when kids are angry, it is important for them to get the anger out physically by hitting pillows, punching bop bags, or doing some physical exercise.
- Take the child for a "walk and talk." This can be helpful for children of any age.

- Spend some one-on-one time with the child. You can work on an art project, go for ice cream, take a drive in the car, or do something he or she wants to do, while also talking through feelings.
- Help the child understand that feelings are okay and that they may have to just sit with them for a bit, even if that is uncomfortable or painful. This is important. You can sit with them and be supportive.
- Some families of faith use prayer. Pray for patience to sit with the feelings and let it be okay, knowing that you are loved and protected.
- Help the child identify other situations in which the child may have felt the same way and give examples of how you as an adult might deal with the same feelings.
- Sometimes with little ones, just holding them and giving comfort while also identifying what they feel will help them calm down and feel safe with their feelings.

When you are empathetic, you help your child become emotionally whole and healthy.

A common perception today is that we are raising entitled children who are too pampered. Empathetic parenting does not mean spoiling children or coddling them or rescuing them from the consequences of bad decisions. It definitely does not mean allowing them to run wild. I strongly believe that healthy families have a hierarchy where the parents are clearly in charge. Without that structure, children cannot feel safe and secure. They need to know that their parents are the bosses who are going to keep them safe and teach them about the world. I am not suggesting that you become your child's best friend or allow children to manipulate you or other people to get their way. I am suggesting, however, that you treat your children's feelings with respect and teach them about their own emotional world. This will help them become healthy adults.

As children learn to manage their feelings and their behavior, they learn about real life. This does not mean you spank, hit, shame, or humiliate them, but that you impose reasonable consequences for disobedience or inappropriate behavior. Parenting children is to teach and guide them to be good people without modeling bad or violent behavior or imposing unreasonable punishments.

What Do I Tell My Child about Their Narcissistic Parent?

As Frans de Waal reminds us in *The Age of Empathy: Nature's Lessons for a Kinder Society*, "Children read 'hearts' well before they read minds."[2] Children recognize people who know how to connect with them. They have antennae for folks who love kids. That means they will sense the emotional void in the narcissistic parent from an early age. They may not know what it is or even how to explain it, but they feel the emptiness and know they are not being heard. It is not appropriate, however, for you to label the other parent a narcissist until the children are older.

It's best for your child if you learn to walk a fine line. Acknowledge what your child is telling you about the other parent but do not defend or vilify that other parent. Children are a part of both of their parents. When you criticize either, the children feel as if you are criticizing them. Even when your children make negative remarks about the other parent, they don't like it when you do.

Don't give voice to your frustration with the other parent in front of your child. Take the high ground. Model the responsible behavior that you want your children to emulate. Refrain from name-calling. If the child speaks to you about something the narcissist parent did that was hurtful, you can speak to the behavior without saying the parent is bad. One client told me, "When my kids come to me and say their dad is being awful to them and they are in distress, I am so tempted to say, 'No shit, Sherlock, why do you think I divorced him?' But, I don't do that, I usually just listen to them and empathize."

Another example is when the children see their narcissistic parent treat others badly—for instance, in restaurants or in public. When they tell you about it, rather than disparaging the other parent, simply tell your children that you don't believe in treating people like that and you are sorry they had to witness it. You might even say that you hope their other parent will learn about this and not do it again. In this way, you support the child's feelings and their perception of reality without putting the other parent down.

I don't need to tell you that narcissists mess with your perception of reality. As you raise your children, it's going to be important to find ways to validate their perception of reality even when the narcissistic parent is trying to push an alternate reality.

A lesbian client named Dora described what happened when she brought her three-year-old daughter, Sofia, to her former partner Ariana's office for a visit. "Ariana said, 'Oh, Sofia, I'm so glad to see you. I missed you so much. Climb into my lap and give me a kiss and a hug.' Sofia did so. Just as she was doing so, Ariana's secretary walked in. Ariana said to her secretary, 'Look at Sofia. She missed me so much, she can't stop hugging me.' Sofia said, 'No, Mommy. You asked me to give you a hug and a kiss.' I was so proud of Sofia! She was totally grounded in reality. I don't know if someone who wasn't familiar with this kind of behavior would understand what was going on, but it was classic Ariana redefining reality to make herself look better. I had a quiet moment with Sofia before I left, and I said to her, 'You know, honey, you were right. Ariana did ask you for that hug and kiss.'"

When Bad Behavior Crosses the Line

In time, the children figure out that their narcissistic parent has a problem. They learn not to make themselves vulnerable to the narcissistic parent and rarely discuss feelings with him or her. They save it all for you! You do carry the burden of the psychological parent and all that entails.

Your children will tell you on many occasions that the other parent ignored them or controlled them in ways they did not like. Where you draw the line is physical and sexual abuse. Talk with your children about what kind of behavior is never okay for anyone to do to them. Explain what they should tell you, and when they should call 911. Emphasize to them that it is okay to report abusive behavior and what they need to do to protect themselves. If the ex-spouse has an alcohol or addiction problem, be honest with your children about some of the risks this creates—for instance, the danger they are in if a parent drives them somewhere while under the influence of drugs or alcohol.

In cases of documented abuse of children, visitations are usually supervised or sometimes stopped completely, but not always. All parents should educate their children in age-appropriate ways about "good touch, bad touch." If your ex-spouse has been abusive to the children, it is even more critical to educate them about physical and sexual abuse.

Emotional Abuse of Children

You may wonder about emotional abuse. Should you report emotional or verbal abuse? Where does it cross the line?

If there is significant emotional abuse of the children and it is causing them angst, get them in therapy to discuss this with a trained professional. In many cases emotional abuse needs to be reported to your local social service agency. If the child is in therapy, the therapist can often help with this. If a custody evaluator is examining the child, this person should know about the verbal and emotional abuse. The therapist can report to the evaluator as well.

Emotional abuse is more difficult to prove as it is not as concrete as a broken arm or a bruise. The judicial system seems to be getting better at understanding the impact of emotional abuse, but the psychological damage caused by narcissistic parents can be difficult to explain and understand. Let me give an example.

When my client Samantha was first dating Mark, she had offered to supervise Mark's five-year-old daughter, Gigi, while Gigi took her bath. Samantha remembered, "I was getting ready to wash Gigi's hair and she started to get upset. She said, 'You have to be very careful with my hair, because it's really thin.' As I was lathering the shampoo into her hair, she started to cry. She said, 'My hair is going to fall out.' And then she changed to being scared. She said, 'Please, please don't tell my dad. Don't tell him I got upset.' It was baffling. It was only later that I understood that Mark was all about appearances. He'd gotten poor Gigi convinced that there was something wrong with her hair. And the other thing was that if Gigi got upset about anything, his response was to get really, really angry with her for being upset."

I once attended a social gathering with friends, family, strangers, and a bunch of cute kids. As the day ended and good-byes were shared, I overheard a six-year-old quietly ask her mother for something. Suddenly, in front of the crowd, the mother exploded and yelled hysterically at the child. The little girl was silenced with tears streaming down her cheeks. It looked like a familiar scene for mother and daughter. The crowd hushed, too, but quickly acted as if nothing had happened.

You wouldn't be able to take either of these stories to court to prove emotional abuse. Instead you have to focus your efforts on helping your children learn how they can help themselves.

How Do I Teach My Children to Set Boundaries with a Narcissistic Parent?

Teaching your children how to be assertive and speak up is important. If they learn how to be assertive early in life, they will be less likely to be aggressive when they get older. They need to share their feelings, even with the narcissistic parent, when something is clearly not okay with them. Their learning how to do so may take some time and even some therapy. They will not want to get in trouble with that parent and could also be fearful of doing this. If the child is faced with an abusive parent, however, the child must learn to report it to you or to the authorities.

You can teach your children how to make *I* statements, just as you learned to do, so they express their own thoughts or feelings and do not tell their mom or dad what to do. For example:

- "I feel sad when you don't listen to me."
- "I feel mad when you make promises and don't keep them."
- "I feel confused when you come to my soccer game but you won't come to my church choir."
- "I feel scared when you yell at Mommy on the phone."

My associate started working with a young child right after a divorce. The child was begging and pleading not to go to visitations with her mother. Working on assertiveness in therapy, this young child progressed nicely. She began as a shy, intimidated, withdrawn child who hid rather than said what she was feeling. With therapy she learned to identify her feelings and express them. This, in turn, increased her self-esteem. The work began with the child practicing assertiveness with safe adults such as her teachers and father. Then she progressed to peers and eventually was able to be assertive with her mother. She had to learn to trust herself and to separate herself from her mother.

Narcissists don't respect boundaries, so you may need to be creative. I had a teenage client who said to his mom, "Can we just have a rule in this house that when Dad calls, we don't pick up the phone? I want to choose when I call him." His mom said, "We can make that a house rule, but help me understand why you want to do it that way. How is it going to help you?" Her son said, "I just never know what to expect when Dad calls. Sometimes it's a really quick phone call about something small. Sometimes he is calling to say he is proud about something I did. But sometimes when I pick up the phone, he just lights into me. I really hate it when that comes out of nowhere. If I can pick and choose the time that I call him back, then I can brace myself to be prepared for anything."

How Do I Help My Child Not Internalize Negative Messages?

No matter what you do as the other parent, your kids are likely to internalize negative messages such as "I'm not good enough," "I'm not okay the way I am," "I am valued for what I do and not for who I am," "I'm only lovable if I do what that parent wants," "It doesn't matter what I say, I am invisible." Your job is to watch for any red flags and always work the other side to offset the negative messages.

The more discussions you can have about these negative messages the better. Rather than bring them up as something the child is internalizing from the other parent, bring them up as general questions to discuss. This will help your child be aware of when they are absorbing the negativity about themselves. For example, you simply ask, "Do you ever feel valued just for your achievements in this family and not for who you really are?" Or . . . "Do you feel your family knows the real you?" "Do you feel we are hearing you?" These discussions may bring the problems to the forefront so you know what you need to address to empower your child. I hope you can see how you can do this without disparaging the other parent.

How Do I Teach My Child to Get Out of the Middle?

Even in the best of divorces, children are often messengers between their parents. Having worked with children of divorce for years, I can tell you *children hate this* and often don't know what to do about it. When the parents are battling, the children cannot please both parents. Placing them in the middle leaves them feeling lost and alone, wondering what to do. Don't put them in this position, please, even in the smallest of ways.

First, don't be the guilty one. Second, when the child carries a message from the other parent, don't take the message. If you do, you are enabling the behavior to continue.

This will come up again and again. Your ex wants to change the visitation schedule for the weekend and tells the children he or she will pick them up earlier and to tell you this. The child must learn to say no. The parents must stop this. Or a parent plans a vacation and tells the child but does not check with the other parent. It comes to the parent through the child. "We are going to Disneyland with Mom!" In this case, the father knew nothing about it, as the mother did not work this through with the coparent.

When things happen, you simply say over and over, "You are not our messenger, and your mom or dad needs to talk to me directly. Don't worry about it. I will handle this." If you do this right away, it will be easier on the child. If you have allowed it to go on, it will be more difficult to change as the child may become used to it. You still need to change it. Always deal directly with the other parent. The more you do this, the more likely the child and the narcissist will understand that communication will not be going through the child no matter what.

This cowardly behavior is not fair to kids. The adults cannot expect the child to be the mediator between them. In reality, professional mediators are adults with graduate-school training. Even they have trouble with narcissists. Don't expect a child of any age to do this.

Here is where their assertiveness training will be handy, too. The children need to be encouraged to say they cannot take a message to the other parent. You can help them by praising them if they call *you* out on putting them in the middle! I have worked with many children who are willing to be the message kid because they believe if they carry messages, it will cut down on the conflict between their parents.

Emma was five years old when I asked her what her top three wishes were and she responded:

- "I wish my mommy would listen to me."
- "I wish my mommy would stop being so mean to my daddy."
- "I wish my parents could talk to each other and not want me to be the mailman to give them stuff from each other."

Normally when I ask five-year-olds that question, they say things like "I want to learn to fly," "I want to be a princess in a castle," "I want a lot of money to buy all the toys in the world," "I want free ice cream for the whole world."

When Eric, age eleven, was asked specifically about his wishes about his parents' divorce, he said:

- "I wish my dad was dead so I could move on with my life."
- "I wish I had a different family that did not fight."
- "I wish I could go away and just escape."

After being trapped in the middle of his parents' battles for six years, this eleven-year-old child was bordering on suicide.

When Do I Take My Child to Therapy?

I think it is a good idea to have children in divorce-adjustment therapy, but if you are divorcing a narcissist, it is a necessity. Often children of high-conflict divorces are court-ordered to attend therapy or strongly encouraged to do so. Therapy allows children to have an uninvolved, nonbiased person to talk to about both parents and the difficult divorce. In talking to a child therapist, they do not have to worry about hurting their parents' feelings or getting in trouble for what they say. A therapist can help them deal with what is going on and help them in adjusting to different homes and different styles of parenting. Adult children of narcissistic parents often talk about the distress they felt as kids when adults did not believe their stories. Conversely, they said how life-affirming it was when they encountered an adult who listened to them and believed them.

When trying to decide about whether to seek therapy for your child, some red flags to watch for include the following: signs of sadness or depression, increased anxiety, poor schoolwork, lack of motivation, aggressive behaviors, regression to baby behaviors, peer conflict, sleep or appetite issues, excessive crying or moodiness, low self-esteem, isolation behaviors, excessive sibling fighting, or any significant change in behavior.

If you can't afford individual therapy for your child, look for divorce groups for children in your community. It can be helpful for children to be around other kids in their same situation. Nonprofit groups offer divorce-adjustment sessions for children. Another place to look is at your child's school. Sometimes the school psychologist or social worker will run a divorce group. These kinds of groups may not understand the dynamics of narcissism, but they still offer an outlet for your child. You might provide the leader some information on narcissism if you feel that is necessary.

You may have difficulty getting your child into any kind of therapy because the other parent objects. Most therapists nationwide have to get consent from both parents to treat a child when the court has mandated joint decision-making in the divorce. Getting this consent is torturous when it involves a narcissist. For narcissists, therapy is not about experience or comfort for the child; it is about whether the therapist is going to see things the narcissist's way. This is yet one more arena in which narcissists like to play games. They usually do not want their children in therapy because they suspect the child may say something bad about them. They typically don't like therapy in general and won't agree to allow most therapists to work with their children. If the child does get treatment, the narcissistic parent usually wants to change therapists quickly, especially when the therapist does not agree with the narcissist's views and acts as an advocate for the child. The narcissistic parent hates to pay part of the costs of treatment and often tries to convince the child that therapy is not needed so it can end quickly. As mentioned earlier, you may need to get a court order.

The therapist will need to start by getting a good history, and you will be asked to provide that background and describe your concerns about the child. The therapist will likely want to do individual intakes with both you and your ex. The consent for treatment is usually signed in this process.

You must recognize that the child therapist is not a custody evaluator and usually cannot testify for you regarding visitation or parenting time. This is because the child therapist is not evaluating both parents, their emotional states, or home environments the way the parenting-time evaluators do. But, the child therapist can be helpful in discussing the emotional and behavioral issues that the children are dealing with related to the divorce. This can be helpful, as the child therapist can pass along this information to your evaluators or even testify about the children's emotional state in court. Also, if the child does not want to see one of the parents or the visits have been stopped or supervised, the child therapist can prepare the child for eventual visitation and reunification with that parent.

When you choose a child therapist, it is wise to find someone who is educated about narcissism and its effects on children as well as experienced in forensic interviewing of children who have endured trauma. Well-trained and experienced therapists know how to help children talk and express feelings and do not ask them leading questions. For children who are at this stage of healing I don't advocate hiring someone who specializes in play therapy. To heal, the child should talk about the issues and not just play them out with toys. An additional danger here is that the play therapist makes subjective assessments based on the play, which are not useful for court testimony or reports as they may be incorrect. I am not saying that play therapy is not a useful therapeutic tool for children, but it is more useful later in processing trauma after all disclosures and diagnoses are complete.

This is a strong bias of mine. I have seen many cases where children have not been protected by play therapy. When children can talk, they can usually tell you what happened to them. They may not be great at giving you peripheral details such as times, dates, and locations, but they can tell you what happened in their age-appropriate language. Choose a therapist who knows how to do this. Otherwise, important issues can be missed and abuse can continue.

When Should I Go Back to Court?

What's right and necessary depends on your child. Your child may be miserable at visitations or overnights, complaining about it, and asking you to help. Returning to court is a big decision and should always be discussed with your attorney and any professionals involved in the case.

The for-sure time to go back to court is when your child is being abused or harmed. Then it is a no-brainer. You have to protect the child. It is more difficult with emotional abuse or neglect, but here professionals can be of assistance to you.

Sometimes a judge will be open to listening to the child alone in chambers. This is not common, however. Most judges do not want to involve children in the court, and rightly so because it puts them smack in the middle of having to choose sides. Your attorney may know the style and preference of your judge. It is worth asking if the judge will hear the child in chambers. One judge I interviewed for this book said that when children were of driving age, he was more likely to let them decide where to spend their time. In one case in our practice, the children were allowed to speak to the judge after five years of custody and visitation battles. They were thrilled to know that they could finally be heard, and they had a lot to say.

In general, though, unless necessary, it is best that you keep your children out of the conversations about court. They should not know when you go to court, what is happening, etc. It is too stressful for them, and they don't understand it until they are at least teenagers. Even then, it puts more stress on them to know these details of your case.

If you want a reality check, ask young kids what they know about court. I did this recently with one of my granddaughters when she was about eight. Here are the questions I asked her and the answers she gave:

- What is a lawyer? "Oh, those guys that wear black suits and yell. They seem to be followers, not leaders."
- What is a judge? "Oh, they pound hammers. I don't know what they are building, but they also yell at people when they do wrong things."
- What is court? "A place you play basketball?"

We smile when we read these innocent answers, but many times children of high-conflict divorce are educated far beyond their years about judges, attorneys, and court. I would rather have children keep their naive nature and not be pulled into adult battlegrounds such as the courtroom.

Trauma and Brain Development in Children

Traumatic experiences, abuse, and neglect have an adverse effect on children's brain development. As the child matures, the developing brain changes in response to the child's environment. Dr. Bruce Perry, an internationally recognized authority on brain development and children in crisis, has done pioneering research in this arena. His research shows that a child's brain develops in sequence, just like other aspects of physical development. Dr. Perry says the sensitive brain of an infant or young child is malleable. Powerful experiences alter the functioning of an adult brain, but for children, especially young children, traumatic events may change the brain's very framework.[3]

Child abuse has far-reaching effects. "Each year, more than 1.25 million children are abused or neglected in the United States, with that number expanding to at least 40 million per year worldwide."[4] Many studies show that children are at greater risk for developing a wide range of physical conditions as well as psychiatric disorders if abused. To raise good people, we must continue to find ways to keep children safe. The more we understand, the closer we come to providing the proper interventions and system changes so badly needed.

Children Witnessing Domestic Violence and Parental Conflict

The US Department of Justice reports that each year 6 million plus children witness domestic violence.[5] If you are a direct victim of domestic violence, you will suffer the long-lasting psychological and sometimes physical effects. If your child has witnessed domestic violence, your child will have secondary trauma that needs to be addressed, too.

Domestic violence is about power and control and involves physical, psychological, and sexual abuse. Only 25 percent of these incidents are reported to the police. One source says that child abuse occurs in 30–60 percent of family violence cases in families with children and that 65 percent of those that abuse their partner also physically or sexually abuse their children.[6]

The effects on children witnessing domestic violence are widespread according to many studies that have focused on children from infancy all through adolescence. Studies show that infants in homes with partner abuse have disrupted attachment, cry excessively, and suffer eating and sleeping problems. They are also at risk for increased physical injury. Preschool children who witness intimate violence may develop a range of problems including psychosomatic complaints such as headaches and abdominal pain, regressive behaviors such as wetting their pants, thumb sucking, and sleep disturbance. They have increased anxiety, whining, crying, and clinging. They sleep poorly and can wake up in terror, manifested by yelling, irritability, hiding, and stuttering.[7]

School-age children can develop headaches and abdominal pain and perform poorly in school. They are less likely to have friends or to participate in outside activities. Their self-esteem and confidence are undermined. They experience guilt and shame and tend to blame themselves.[8]

Adolescents are more likely to have a fatalistic view of the future, resulting in an increased rate of risk taking and antisocial behavior, such as school truancy, early sexual activity, substance abuse, and delinquency.[9]

We see too many children court-ordered after divorces into unsupervised contact with an abusive parent. It is a public health crisis. According to a 2008 article by Joyanna Silberg, PhD, "a conservative estimate by experts at the Leadership Council on Child Abuse and Interpersonal Violence [is that] more than 58,000 children a year are ordered into unsupervised contact with physically or sexually abusive parents following divorce in the United States."[10]

We cannot minimize or discount the damage done to children when they are seeing or experiencing any kind of abuse. We have to work together for the best interests of children and look at new interventions.

The Future of My Children

In summary, the double duty of the normal psychological parent is an immense responsibility. You need help to reverse the damage to your child and do damage control.

Studies show that early identification and intervention with abused and neglected children can influence development in many positive ways. Research shows that the brain is capable of changing in response to experiences, and while we have only focused on the lingering effects of bad experiences, with good professionals helping you, you may be able to use that same malleability to heal traumatic episodes in your child's past.[11]

When you are attuned to your children's emotional world, they will have the opportunity to grow into healthy people. This means we are creating not only a safe physical world but a safe emotional world for them to develop and grow.

I was moved recently by a client who said, "Here I am, fifteen years after the divorce, and I've gotten to a place where I pity my ex. The reason is, she could have had a wonderful life and she blew it. I'm a really decent human being and she drove me away. We have a wonderful daughter. I know that I am blessed to have this child. My ex doesn't understand that. My daughter loves her mom, no matter what, but the older she gets and the more power she has to make decisions for herself, the more she chooses not to spend time with her. My daughter and I have been through a lot of pain, but we have learned and grown from it, and we are blessed to be where we are in our lives."

In the next and last chapter, I will describe some changes that my colleagues and I have found helpful in our practice when working with high-conflict divorce and narcissism. I feel strongly that a bigger system change is needed, including court reform. As you will see, I am going to propose a pilot project to do things differently.

Some of you may decide not to read about the pilot project. I can understand that, even though I would encourage you to look at it. It includes helpful ideas that you can implement by yourself, even within the current system. However, in case you decide to end reading here, I want to leave you with a strong closing message.

The hopeful and encouraging answer to the question "Will I ever be free of you?" is yes, you can be free. You can understand what turned your life upside down and inside out, because now you recognize narcissism and understand its distorting impact. You can break free and rediscover your authentic self because you have a road map in the five steps of recovery. You can free yourself and your children from the legacy of distorted love because you are strong, wise, and loving.

Yes, you can be free.

CHAPTER TEN

The Pilot Project: AIMS

Throughout the book, I have talked about the difficult issues that arise in a divorce when one party is a narcissist. The highly contentious divorce is expensive for the divorcing parties and a burden on the court system, and traumatic for the children and parents. When you add narcissism to the mix, it is even more frustrating, expensive, and traumatic. Who suffers the most in a high-conflict divorce? The children.

We are not doing enough to identify and protect children of high-conflict divorce. When parents use their children as pawns in a divorce, as narcissistic parents often do, they are missing something. As a society that refuses to recognize and address this problem, we are all missing something.

In this chapter, I set out my vision for a new way for the courts to manage high-conflict divorces, using an approach called AIMS. AIMS is an acronym for "Am I missing something?" AIMS also characterizes the mission statement of this approach: "Aiming for the best results for children of high-conflict divorce."

I have written this pilot project based on successful therapeutic strategies we use in our practice. Even without a pilot project in place, you can suggest that your therapist and your attorney consider using some of these approaches in your case, such as child therapy, empathetic parent coaching, and family therapy, to help with the unique issues of high-conflict divorce. The major difference in using these approaches as part of a pilot project is that, with outside funding, a therapeutic team, and the leverage of judicial approval, these tools will work together more efficiently and effectively.

AIMS is designed to help families where one or both parents have shown an impaired ability to empathize with their children. Using the AIMS model, the divorce negotiations are carefully managed by an experienced caseworker who supervises a team of therapists for the individuals involved—both parents, the children, and the family as a whole—as well as coaches to teach the parents how they can become more aware and more empathetic through the divorce. I believe that when dealing with high-conflict divorce, successful therapeutic management is more effective than protracted court battles.

The AIMS model uses therapeutic strategies to accomplish three important goals:

1. Reduce parental conflict in and out of court.
2. Help individual parents improve their parenting and coparenting skills.
3. Advocate in constructive ways to understand and support the children's best interests, with a special focus on their mental health and emotional needs.

The AIMS approach is presented here as a pilot project with a specific protocol. To be implemented, it needs a broad consensus, as well as judicial approval and funding. Not what you would call a piece of cake! But in researching this book, I found widespread agreement that our current system is problematic, as well as a willingness among attorneys, judges, therapists, evaluators, divorcing parents, and their children to try something different.

When I was talking to the legal and mental health professionals who work with divorce, I wondered if the words *narcissism* and *high-conflict divorce* would ring a bell. It turned out that it was more like clashing cymbals. People had strong opinions.

Gail Meinster, a district court judge in Jefferson County, Colorado, says, "The courtroom is no place to solve these kinds of problems. The focus is so often on how to get back at the other parent. They think we will not see through their manipulation. Unfortunately, they're often right about that. We try to craft a compromise but ultimately nobody wins. Attorneys' fees in these cases may reach an exorbitant level, and these cases are incredibly time-consuming for the courts. Judges hate to see children caught in this scenario. Then you add the emotional drain on the judicial officer and the helplessness that goes with it. Sometimes I wonder, what can I possibly order that will help? We take this seriously and really agonize over these cases that involve children."

Magistrate Marianne Marshall Tims, of Jefferson County District Court in Colorado, said that she often tells parents, "Your children are not going to go to college with the cost of this litigation, but your lawyer's children are." She says that judges in other counties get rotated or moved around a lot and most have their round with family law, which they refer to as "pots and pans" court. She says, "It is easier, though, to talk about who gets the pots and pans than who gets Christmas Day with the kids." Our statutes are written about the child's best interest, but Magistrate Tims says the problem with this is that "every parent thinks they alone know best what is in the best interest of their child, and by law they can always weigh in about this. But this becomes a problem when it gets blown out of proportion and the children become pawns in the process. It is a concern when they can get what they want in other issues like property and finances if they use the children. They know the other parent will lie down and give in."

Magistrate Tims said that many of these high-conflict divorce cases come into court every two years until the child is nineteen or beyond. She said that in the beginning it can be difficult to determine which parent is causing problems. By the time a really damaged kid shows up and they can trace it back to the responsible parent, the damage is already done. In discussing the costs of litigation, Tims says the highest cost of divorce she has seen was $250,000, but each motion that is filed could cost $15,000 to each side, so it can be "a thousand dollars a month forever."

Although progress has been made in understanding emotional abuse, Magistrate Tims expressed concern about the children. "The children begin to question their own judgment. They have been told so many lies, their perception of reality is messed up. They learn not to follow their gut, as 'Mommy says Daddy doesn't love me,' or vice versa, 'so it must be that my own judgment is bad.'" She says that sometimes "you keep track as a judge how long the child will have to endure this, and then eventually the kid will vote with his or her feet and just not do it anymore. It is horrible to have to wait for the child to figure it out for themselves."

Magistrate Tims's comments make vivid the damaging, potentially lifelong effects of emotional abuse.

Dr. Andrew Loizeaux, a Denver clinical psychologist who has been doing parental responsibility evaluations (PREs) for twenty-five years, said, "Children with narcissistic parents have trouble advocating for themselves and develop a distorted and compromised sense of self. Their safest strategy is to align with the narcissistic parent because it is self-protective. So they speak and act in ways to either gain the narcissist's approval or avoid the narcissist's wrath. There is diminished attention to their own internal world because they are so focused on the acceptance from the narcissistic parent."

Dr. Loizeaux also said, "Clinicians can be manipulated by narcissists. When you have a savvy narcissist who presents well, who is intelligent and knows how to turn on the charm, then the clinician may be seduced into the narcissist's distorted worldview. On the flip side, narcissists can also be skilled in delivering veiled and implied threats, so a professional may compromise clinical opinions out of fear of the narcissist's retribution."

The courts can also be confused by the complexity of these cases. Barbara Shindell, LCSW, a psychotherapist and forensic evaluator in high-conflict divorce cases, states, "In a lot of ways, these cases are similar to domestic violence cases. The nonnarcissistic parent participates in the battle and becomes dysregulated, and they can look like the problem. Their reaction to the narcissistic parent, the power and control and the trauma, gets them into trouble. It requires a nuanced and systematic analysis of the dynamic to accurately diagnose and treat the family system. The court system often reacts to the behavior rather than the dynamic that produces frantic and dysregulated behaviors that makes the nonnarcissistic parent look like the problem, even in situations where they are not."

When we, as professionals, testify in court in cases where one party is a narcissist, narcissists commonly file grievances and lawsuits against those of us who do not agree with the narcissist's view. When you are testifying, the narcissist's grand goal is to make sure that you, too, the professional, are shown to be "not good enough"!

Another prominent judge described how exasperated judges become with these cases. "It is hard to understand why they can't follow orders, and while we can try to control harassment, stalking, and intimidation, we can't order nurturance. Sometimes the judges think it is their fault that they cannot get the family to function. We don't want repeat customers. We have all had cases with four to five inches of paperwork and hearings every couple of years, plus all the contempts filed. One case got so bad, I had to make decisions on who took the children for the flu shot and who took the children for their vaccinations. Not to mention the case where I had to enter an order on custody of the dog. I actually had to look at the best interest of the dog, and the dog needed a yard."

Magistrate Jason Carrithers, of Jefferson County District Court, Colorado, told me, "We want to problem-solve, but with a narcissist, you know they are going to come back. There is nothing more frustrating than crafting a thoughtful order and then seeing it come back. It feels defeating. We see a lot of conflict around money with narcissistic parents. It is a way to control things. They either buy love or drive the other parent nuts."

The many professionals I interviewed all agreed that these kinds of divorces overwhelm the system, cost thousands of dollars, and make the children suffer terribly. These professionals see the system as part of the problem, yet also believe that it can be part of the solution.

Most of the professionals that I interviewed were receptive to trying out a different approach.

The AIMS protocol is designed to do just that. I modeled it after a successful program already in use in Colorado that was developed for families with a history of sexual abuse. AIMS builds on an approach that has been shown to work well.

What Are the Problems We Are Trying to Fix?

In her 2011 book, *Rebuilding Justice: Civil Courts in Jeopardy and Why You Should Care*, former Colorado Supreme Court justice Rebecca Love Kourlis described an increasing number of litigants representing themselves and more requests for assistance from the court at a time when court resources are shrinking. Judges are unhappy with the process, she wrote, and so are the litigants. As the fights rage on, the children suffer poor school outcomes and fail to integrate into society, which has effects that ripple out from the family and influence society and the economy. "Recognizing the breadth and severity of the problem, it is now time to evaluate new approaches and implement reforms in the court process itself and also establish out of court resources to provide alternative non-adversarial avenues for the resolution of family matters," Justice Kourlis wrote.[1]

High-conflict and contentious divorce also affects everyday work environments and productivity, causing other kinds of problems for families and their employers including:

- High costs for the litigating parents (in my research, I found divorce costs that ranged from $50,000 to $1.2 million).
- A burden on the court system, resulting from parents who cannot agree and parents who cannot follow court orders.
- A difficult situation for judges, who must balance the evidence of experts who do not agree with each other, but may also not have the full picture of what's going on with the family.
- Seasoned professionals leaving the field due to the difficulty of

these cases, the burden of being sued and grieved, and the fear of retribution.

- Contentious and chaotic warfare in and out of the courts.

But even worse, the children in these cases suffer:

- Knowing that their parents are fighting, and that they are the object of the fights.
- Being evaluated over and over by different experts.
- Getting in trouble with a parent for having told the truth to a therapist.
- Not being heard, not having a voice.
- Suffering the trauma of emotional abuse with its lifelong consequences.
- Suffering the trauma of physical or sexual abuse.
- Being left to live in poverty because all their parents' money has been spent on litigation.
- Long-term mental health problems.

Alternative Approaches

Alternative dispute-resolution techniques such as mediation can work wonderfully when you have two reasonable people who truly want what's best for their children. But these kinds of approaches don't work well when one party is not cooperative. Former justice Kourlis and other change advocates are not arguing for a one-size-fits-all solution to current problems. They are arguing that it's time to evaluate new approaches. I will argue that with the AIMS approach a therapeutic team should work with the judicial system.

Why Use a Pilot Project?

While I have strong ideas about how the system could be changed, it won't change until we can prove that things can be done differently.

We have to convince the doubters that the new way produces better outcomes that can be measured, such as fewer court appearances, lower cost to the divorcing parties, and/or healthier children. Experimenting within the boundaries of a pilot project is easier than trying to change a whole system at once. Some people will say, "That will never work!" We can say to those people, "How will we know if we don't try it?" After all, if it's broke, we should fix it! A pilot project is a way to test a fix.

With a pilot project, you can try something for six months or a year and then step back and ask "What worked really well?" and "What did not work so well?" Doing a small pilot project will help us to answer important such questions as which families benefited from the pilot program and which did not. Is getting involved at the beginning of divorce proceedings important? Or can these therapeutic interventions turn things around even after a history of court fighting? We may learn that some of the successes will be in areas that we did not expect. When things don't work out so well, it will be important to learn from those failures. After you have those answers, you can make midcourse corrections and start a second pilot.

The AIMS Pilot Project

MISSION

AIMS will use a new model of therapeutic strategies to reduce parental conflict in and out of court and to improve parenting and coparenting skills in families in a high-conflict divorce. The primary focus will be the children. Its mission will be "Aiming for the best results for children of high-conflict divorce."

WHY NOT USE THE WORD *NARCISSISM*?

You're probably wondering why, after having written an entire book focused on the problems of navigating a high-conflict divorce with a narcissist, I don't use the word *narcissism* for the pilot program. First, we may not have a formal diagnosis of parental narcissism (narcissists don't believe that they have a problem, so they don't seek treatment, right?). Second, it's not helpful to demonize a parent. A parent who feels attacked or made out to be "the bad parent" will not want to participate. While parents probably won't have a choice about participating in the pilot (a court order will likely require them to participate), we will serve the family and the children best if we can identify benefits for *all* parties, including a parent who may be a narcissist. That's why we focus on the children and how they are being affected.

THE TEAM APPROACH

The AIMS protocol would use a team of therapeutic professionals: a case manager, child therapists, two parent coaches, and a family therapist.

Step One: Referral to the AIMS Pilot Program

Divorcing couples with children could be considered for referral to the AIMS Pilot Project if they meet two criteria:

1. A pattern of high conflict with repeated court appearances and interpersonal conflict in and out of the courtroom.
2. One or both parents have demonstrated an inability to empathize with their children, and some evidence suggests that the children are currently suffering emotional distress and will continue to suffer emotional harm.

Only judges and parenting responsibility evaluators (PREs) or child family investigators (CFIs) would be able to make formal referrals to the pilot project. Other individuals could ask a judge, PRE, or CFI to consider referring a family to the pilot project. However, it would be up to judges, PREs, or CFIs to decide if a referral is appropriate. The referral would then be made as a court order from the presiding judge.

Why do I propose setting up the referral process like this? A judge who sees a couple in court over and over sees their contentious dynamics and knows whether court orders are being followed. A PRE or CFI who has done an evaluation of the family will also know about the family issues. Sometimes psychological evaluations of the parents are conducted, which will identify traits that may flag a referral.

Here are some specific questions for the judge or evaluator to ask about a particularly difficult parent who is causing chaos in a divorce to determine if that family would be an appropriate referral to the AIMS Pilot Project. Do we have a parent who:

- Is initiating many court actions?
- Has a pattern of ignoring or disobeying court rulings?
- Blames everyone but himself or herself?
- Never takes accountability?
- Thinks he or she is always right?
- Seems to be out of touch with his or her own feelings?
- Does not seem able to tune in to the feelings of his or her child or children?
- Does not get over things?
- Pursues power at all costs?
- Never seems to be focused on what is best for the children, but rather on his or her own issues and interests—money, property, time, parenting time?
- Seems overly worried about what his or her children are going to say and how it reflects on him or her? Or how the children's appearance or behavior reflects on him or her?
- Is always telling other people how to do their jobs?
- Indicates by demeanor, words, or threats that others (such as the judges, therapists, or evaluators) are "not good enough"?
- Never asks how anyone else is doing?
- Tends to go on and on about how great he or she is and how awful the other parent is?
- Lies?

- Manipulates other people to get his or her way?
- Tells different people different stories about the same incident?
- Seems more focused and interested on what his or her children do than who they are as people?
- Seems to mistrust everyone?
- Does not spend significant amounts of quality time with his or her children?
- Goes to the children's events and activities only if he or she has a particular interest in the activity?
- Pushes the child to be involved only in things or activities he or she likes?
- Does not seem to have a value system to live by?
- Still wants to exploit the ex-spouse, even after the divorce is ancient history?
- Never calmed down after the divorce?
- Seems to have no qualms about using the children as pawns in battles with the ex-spouse?
- Is dangerous in any way, has ever had a restraining order placed against him or her, or has a criminal record?

In looking at how the children interact with this parent, do we see children who:

- Do not seem comfortable with this parent?
- Do not share feelings with this parent?
- Love the parent, but are reluctant to spend time with him or her?
- Seem to be constantly trying to gain this parent's love and approval without success?

In feedback from other witnesses in the case, are people saying this parent:

- Is all about image and how things look to others?
- Is constantly trying to charm or impress others?

- Is demonstrating exploitative behavior or actions designed to exert power or control over others?

Step Two: Assignment to a Case Manager

As soon as a court order is in place compelling the family to participate in the AIMS project, the family will be assigned to the case manager, who is familiar with both the therapeutic and judicial processes, has superb communication skills, and has special training in the AIMS protocol.

I have included detailed job descriptions for the case manager and other participants in the program at the end of this chapter. To hit the high points, the case manager would be responsible for:

- Making the referrals for each member of the family to the participating professionals who have been trained in the protocol.
- Obtaining releases from both parents or from the supervising judge allowing the children to participate in the program.
- Obtaining releases from both parents and the supervising judge allowing the members of the therapeutic team to talk with each other and with the presiding judge.
- Setting monthly meetings for the professional team.
- Establishing goals, monitoring progress, and keeping track of performance against the benchmarks established for the pilot program.
- Reporting back to the judge quarterly.

Step Three: Therapy Referrals

The case manager will refer the family members to child therapists, coaches for the parents, and a family therapist, all of whom will work together as a team. It would be helpful for several therapists in each pilot community to be trained in the AIMS protocol so that participating families have several therapists to choose from to ensure a therapeutic alliance and good fit.

THE CHILD THERAPIST

I've talked before about the important and supportive role a child therapist can play in divorce. In the therapist's office the children can feel safe asking questions and discussing important feelings that they may not feel comfortable discussing with their parents. Children find it helpful to be able to talk about their feelings, fears, parental loyalties, changes in their lives, custody, and visitation issues with an objective adult.

When a divorce is high conflict or when children have a parent unable to empathize with them, a good child therapist is even more important. A therapist who understands the harmful short- and long-term impacts of impaired parenting can help the children develop coping tools that they may use over a lifetime.

To participate in the AIMS pilot, a child therapist would need expertise in high-conflict divorce and the emotional impact of having a parent who is not able to empathize with a child. This therapist would give children of different ages an emotional tool kit to deal with that parent. They would also need to have special training in the AIMS pilot protocols.

When possible, it is better to have just one child therapist for all the children. One therapist seeing several children in a family will develop an especially nuanced understanding of the family dynamics. Also, because of the program's requirements to communicate and coordinate among different therapists, fewer therapists would make for easier communication and better team unity.

In some cases, visits to one parent may have been stopped or may occur only under close supervision, or a child may resist seeing or refuse to see one parent. In those cases, the child therapist will prepare the child for eventual visitation and reunification with that parent and report back to the case manager and larger team when the child is ready.

PARENT COACH ONE (PC1)

I have called the first parenting coach PC1. This coach will teach the parent who is not attuned to the child's feelings how to validate, communicate, and listen, which are all basic skills of being a good parent. This therapist's primary responsibility lies in coaching parent one in the full repertoire of empathetic parenting skills. This is a distinctly different role from providing therapy oriented toward overall personal growth and understanding.

PARENT COACH TWO (PC2)

The second parenting coach, called PC2, will coach the parent who is able to empathize with the children, but who is suffering from the trauma of both the marriage and the divorce. This coach should have experience in trauma work, but will also assist this parent to develop the skills to parent extra empathetically and to support their children in areas such as setting effective boundaries. Thus the work here will be supportive and educational as well as trauma focused.

In some families both parents lack empathy; in those cases, both parents will receive coaching that is heavily focused on empathetic parenting skills.

THE FAMILY THERAPIST

While the family therapist will be a member of the therapeutic team from the beginning, he or she will not begin to treat family members together until the individual therapists and the entire therapeutic team feel that the necessary groundwork has been done in individual therapy. The therapeutic team will refer family members to the family therapist for specific services such as:

Clarification sessions—used when a parent has a history of having abused a child. These sessions bring the difficult parent and the child together with the assistance of the family therapist. The parenting coach and the child therapist may need to be a part of these sessions as determined by the team. The child will have an opportunity to discuss his or her feelings with this parent in a safe therapeutic setting. These sessions also will be used to hold the parent accountable for his or her behavior, to allow that parent to apologize to the child, and to discuss what he or she has learned in their parent coach sessions.

Reunification sessions—these will be used in situations when a child has not been having visitations with a parent.

Coparent therapy—after two successful clarification sessions, the family therapist will move to family therapy with both parents, discussing communication, visitation, and any issues that need to be resolved between the parents in order to avoid litigation. If the parents cannot reach agreement on specific issues, then the therapeutic team will make a recommendation to the judge based on what the team believes to be in the children's best interests.

Family therapy—after reunification sessions and coparent therapy, the family therapist will meet with the whole family. Family therapy will continue as long as the family therapist and the team think it is necessary for the emotional well-being of the children. These sessions will allow the family therapist to teach the entire family about post-divorce life and adjustment. Any remaining issues will be addressed.

Step Four: The Therapeutic Team

The therapeutic team will hold monthly meetings, facilitated by the case manager, to discuss their individual clients' progress and the family's progress. They will also identify any issues that require judicial action and make a team recommendation on those issues.

The case manager will submit a monthly report to the supervising judge, updating the judge on any important developments or changes and conveying team recommendations. For example, in cases with visitation problems, the therapeutic team might agree on rebuilding the parent-child relationship in stages, starting with supervised visitation, moving on to unsupervised community visitation just before a family therapy session, followed by longer visits. Changes to visitation or parenting time still rest with the judge.

Step Five: Maintenance

The other therapists will continue to work individually with their clients as long as is needed, but the family therapist will stay on board to assist the family with future issues. The family therapist will continue to report to the case manager. When new issues emerge, all therapists can be brought back on board, but the family therapist will always be consulted to see if there can be family resolution.

What Are the Benefits of This Therapeutic Strategy?

This therapeutic strategy will:

- Assist judges by giving them important and expanded information on which to base their decisions.
- Allow judges to make decisions based on consensus recommendations from a therapeutic team, rather than having to sort through competing recommendations from different experts.
- Allow judges to move these kinds of cases from the high stakes of a litigation courtroom to a judicially managed process supported by therapeutic recommendations.
- Streamline the process for families and children, cutting down on contentious and chaotic warfare.
- Protect the confidentiality of children's therapy records and get rid of a particular problem in the current approach, where a parent has the opportunity to hear in court what a child has said about the parent in therapy. In many cases where this has resulted in a parent's becoming angry at a child, it also results in children learning that they should not trust therapists.
- Address the problem of seasoned professionals leaving the

field because of narcissists' or angry parents' retribution. It will be harder to grieve and sue a whole team of professionals.

- Allow for better continuity of care for the family.
- Cut down on repeated requests for additional evaluations of the children.
- Reduce the number of continued hearings that go nowhere because a parent does not follow court orders.
- Allow for less "splitting" of the professionals involved in these kinds of cases
- Give children some special therapeutic care where care is badly needed.

How Might This Program Be Funded?

I'm sure you have been asking yourself, how would this program be funded and how would the therapeutic team be paid? I believe this puzzle could be solved in various ways depending on your court and your resources as a community. I also believe it takes some thinking outside the box and some hard work.

There's probably no single answer. Some health insurance plans will cover mental health care. It will be worthwhile to explore grant programs. (I know that the American Psychological Association provided a grant to fund a pilot parenting-coordinator project in Washington, DC, where services were provided pro bono to needy families.) In some districts, judicial money is available for pilot projects. But, given the money that is spent on divorce, court hearings, and attorneys, I also think this program could be funded by the parties of divorce and be much less expensive for them in the long run, as well as help them solve the significant issues.

One possibility I would like to look at in Colorado would be to set up a nonprofit organization that would help fund the AIMS project for those families who could not afford these services. A nonprofit organization could assist in the pilot project with a sliding fee depending on the income of the family.

I think the ultimate solution would be to combine judicial funds, nonprofit funds, and income of families who need help. More will come on the funding issue as we continue development of this pilot project.

How to Determine Project Success

Any pilot project needs a way to determine success, failure, weaknesses, and strengths. It's important to compare the pilot project's performance to the traditional way of doing things. It appears we already have a control group of families as we have been working with high-conflict divorce for quite some time and have seen the outcomes. Some possible factors to measure success would be the following:

- Court time and costs at the judicial level.
- Total cost of divorce for the families.
- Number of times in court hearings.
- Family satisfaction and outcomes (surveys or clinical interviews).
- Numbers of evaluations of children.
- Assessment by the therapeutic team based on professional experience.
- Time spent on AIMS cases versus other cases from the judicial bench.
- Mental health assessments of the children.
- Quality of parents' communication.

Expanding the Pilot with a Financial Mediator?

One of the people whom I asked to review this pilot-project proposal was an attorney with decades of experience. He asked if I would consider adding a financial mediator to the team. I felt this was too ambitious for the initial program. However, if the pilot was successful, this would be worth considering. If high-conflict parents can learn to communicate more effectively about their children, then that better communication might be extended to the property and financial issues in a divorce.

Getting Judicial Approval

A pilot project such as AIMS would need judicial approval. As I have investigated this process, I have learned that developing a pilot will differ in each jurisdiction or community. It is probably best to find a district or chief judge who would like to experiment with such a program. It would then be necessary to put together a detailed and compelling proposal and seek judicial approval.

Summary of AIMS

Although a big undertaking, the pilot project proposed here is just a beginning to solutions needed for divorce when a difficult parent is stirring up conflict. I hope this proposal will be a springboard for more development, discussion, and future projects that will help children in the long run. You may be wondering how this can help you now. Examine this new approach for elements that you can implement on your own, or ask a judge to order some of these elements as part of your divorce settlement. As a professional or a party of divorce, you may be inspired to consider implementing an AIMS pilot program in your community.

Rescuing children stuck on the battlefield of divorce creates a victory for all. If you are a party of divorce, know that my heart is with you, and I will continue on my mission for the much-needed change in this area of mental health, court reform, and high-conflict divorce.

Job Descriptions for the Therapeutic Team

AIMS PILOT PROJECT
CASE MANAGER JOB DESCRIPTION

Roles and Responsibilities

The case manager for the AIMS Pilot Project will be responsible for coordinating the provision of timely and appropriate services to each family referred to the AIMS Pilot Project. Additionally, the case manager will schedule meetings of the therapeutic team and will provide the supervising judge with periodic progress reports. This position requires exceptional communication and organizational skills. The case manager will report to the supervising judge.

The case manager will have the following responsibilities:

- Schedule and conduct the initial intake interview with parents referred to AIMS. Explain the purpose, goals, and structure of the program. Obtain all necessary forms, documents, and releases from each parent. Seek assistance from the supervising judge as necessary (for instance, request an order for child therapy if one or both parents are unwilling to sign releases).

- Determine the resources that are needed for the therapeutic team based on the size of the family and any family-specific issues. Provide each parent with the names of approved participating therapists. Establish and communicate required time frames for initial therapeutic appointments.

- Schedule and facilitate a monthly meeting of the therapeutic team to discuss progress. Take minutes of those meetings and report back to the supervising judge.

- Monitor each family member's participation in the project; alert the team if individual family members are not participating. Ensure that established pilot project benchmarks are measured at the appropriate times.

- Track the resources used/expenses of the program for each family.

Qualifications

The successful candidate will be an exceptionally well-organized person with strong oral and written communication skills. It is critically important that this person have demonstrated an ability to facilitate the work of multidisciplinary teams and to work well with all sorts of people.

The successful candidate will be trained in the AIMS model.

AIMS PILOT PROJECT MATERIALS DEVELOPED BY KARYL MCBRIDE, PH.D

AIMS PILOT PROJECT
CHILD THERAPIST JOB DESCRIPTION

Roles and Responsibilities

The child therapist will work as a member of the therapeutic team in the AIMS Pilot Project.

Responsibilities will include providing therapy to children whose families are participating in the AIMS Pilot Project, attending monthly meetings with the therapeutic team, and providing periodic written progress reports. The child therapist will attend clarification or family sessions with the child as needed.

Qualifications

To be considered for this position, a candidate must be licensed as a mental health professional and have additional training and experience in child therapy.

Additionally, candidates will be asked to show that they have training and/or experience in the following specific areas:

- Developmental needs of children.
- Divorce adjustment for children.
- Diagnosis and treatment of the narcissistic family system, with expertise in the problems that arise for children when a parent or parents are narcissistic.
- Forensic training on how to interview and talk to children without asking leading questions or exerting undue influence.
- Working with children who have experienced trauma.
- Understanding the effects of trauma on children, PTSD, and recovery.
- An understanding of the benefits and limitations of play therapy—specifically, an understanding that play therapy is not appropriate when children are at risk for physical or sexual abuse.

The successful candidate will be trained in the AIMS model.

AIMS PILOT PROJECT MATERIALS DEVELOPED BY KARYL MCBRIDE, PH.D.

AIMS PILOT PROJECT
PARENT COACH ONE (PC1) JOB DESCRIPTION

Roles and Responsibilities

Parent coach one (PC1) will work as a member of the therapeutic team in the AIMS Pilot Project. He or she will be assigned to the parent who was referred to the program because a judge or parenting time evaluator found that this parent could not show empathy for his or her child or showed a pattern of behavior that was not in the child's best interest. PC1 will assist this parent to learn how to tune in to the child's feelings and to parent with empathy. This therapy will focus on teaching the validation, communication, and listening skills inherent to being a good parent.

Responsibilities will include providing therapy to the first parent, attending monthly meetings with the therapeutic team, and providing written reports monthly or as requested by the case manager or presiding judge. PC1 will attend clarification or family sessions with his or her client as needed.

Qualifications

To be considered for this position, a candidate must be licensed as a mental health professional.

Additionally, candidates will be asked to show that they have training and/or experience in the following specific areas:

- Divorce adjustment in adults.
- Diagnosis and treatment of narcissism spectrum disorders.
- Diagnosis and treatment of the narcissistic family system, with expertise in the problems that arise for children when a parent is or parents are narcissistic.
- Teaching parenting skills, especially empathetic parenting.
- Teaching anger management.

The successful candidate will be trained in the AIMS model.

AIMS PILOT PROJECT MATERIALS DEVELOPED BY KARYL MCBRIDE, PH.D

AIMS PILOT PROJECT
PARENT COACH TWO (PC2) JOB DESCRIPTION

Roles and Responsibilities

Parent coach two (PC2) will work as a member of the therapeutic team in the AIMS Pilot Project. He or she will be assigned to the parent who was referred to the program because the parent's spouse was abusive verbally, mentally, physically, or sexually. This therapeutic work will be trauma based and focused on trauma resolution and support.

Responsibilities will include providing therapy to the second parent, attending monthly meetings with the therapeutic team, and providing written reports monthly or as requested by the case manager or presiding judge. PC2 will attend clarification or family sessions with his or her client as needed.

Qualifications

To be considered for this position, a candidate must be licensed as a mental health professional.

Additionally, candidates will be asked to show that they have training and/or experience in the following specific areas:

- Divorce adjustment in adults.
- Diagnosis and treatment of narcissism spectrum disorders.
- Trauma-based therapy and trauma resolution.
- Diagnosis and treatment of the narcissistic family system, with expertise in the problems that arise for children when a parent is or parents are narcissistic.
- Teaching parenting skills, especially empathetic parenting.

The successful candidate will be trained in the AIMS model.

AIMS PILOT PROJECT MATERIALS DEVELOPED BY KARYL MCBRIDE, PH.D

AIMS PILOT PROJECT
FAMILY THERAPIST JOB DESCRIPTION

Roles and Responsibilities

The family therapist will work as a member of the therapeutic team in the AIMS Pilot Project. He or she will be asked to participate in the team when it is first established and will attend the monthly progress meetings. However, the family therapist will not begin to see members of the family in therapy until the child therapist and parent coaches have determined that clarification or family therapy is appropriate.

The family therapist may be asked to lead clarification sessions — sessions that may be needed for the difficult parent and the child to discuss any issues that need resolution, with the child's needs being the primary focus. These sessions may also include the child therapist and/or one of the parent coaches. Additionally, the family therapist may also be asked to lead reunification sessions — sessions that may be needed for a child and a parent who have not seen each other for some time, or who have seen each other only during supervised visitation.

After individual issues are resolved, the family therapist will be the unifying therapist for the family. The family therapist may conduct coparenting sessions with the parents before working with the entire family. Family therapy is designed as a final therapeutic strategy to set out clear ground rules and boundaries for coparenting and for ongoing visitation and/or parenting time.

Qualifications

To be considered for this position, a candidate must be licensed as a marriage and family therapist.

Additionally, candidates will be asked to show that they have training and/or experience in the following specific areas:

- Divorce adjustment issues for children and parents.
- Family therapy.
- Childhood abuse.
- Understand and know how to teach and model empathetic parenting.
- Setting up regulated and sequential visitation time if needed.

Finally, the family therapist will be asked to make a commitment to stay available as needed to assist with future family disputes.

AIMS PILOT PROJECT MATERIALS DEVELOPED BY KARYL MCBRIDE, PH.D

Intake Forms for the
AIMS Pilot Project

Intake Date:

AIMS PILOT PROJECT
PARENT INTAKE FORM

Name and Address of Parent Completing Form

Name (Last, First, MI):

Date of Birth:	Age:	Sex:

Current Address:

City:	State:	Zip Code:

Telephone and E-mail Contact Information

Home:	Work:	Cell:

E-mail:

Employment Information

Employer:

Job Title:

Information Relative to Current Court Proceedings

Case Name:

Case Docket Number:

Judge:

Parenting Responsibility Evaluator (PRE) or Child Family Investigator (CFI):

Your Attorney's Name and Contact Information:

Name and Address of Other Parent in Current Court Proceedings

Name (Last, First, MI):

Date of Birth:	Age:	Sex:

Current Address:

City:	State:	Zip Code:

Telephone and E-mail Contact Information

Home:	Work:	Cell:

E-mail:

Employment Information

Employer:

Job Title:

Children

Name	Age	Relationship to You

Other Household Members

Name	Age	Relationship to You

Abbreviated Medical History

Your Primary-Care Physician's Name and Contact Information:

Health Problems:

Medications:

Previous or Current Counseling:

Psychiatric Hospitalizations:

Is there currently a restraining order in effect or has a restraining order ever been issued against you?

Additional Information

Payment Arrangements

Fee per Session:

Method of Payment:

Insurance Coverage:

Therapist:

Circle: PC1   PC2   Family Therapist

Intake Date:

AIMS PILOT PROJECT
CHILD INTAKE FORM

Name and Address of Child

Name (Last, First, MI):		

Date of Birth:	Age:	Sex:

Current Address:

City:	State:	Zip Code:

Information Relative to Current Court Proceedings

Case Name:

Case Docket Number:

Judge:

Parenting Responsibility Evaluator (PRE) or Child Family Investigator (CFI):

Child's Attorney or Guardian ad Litem (if applicable):

Parent 1 Information—   Circle   Mother   Father

Name (Last, First, MI):

Date of Birth:	Age:	Sex:

Current Address:

City:	State:	Zip Code:

Telephone and E-mail Contact Information

Home:	Work:	Cell:

E-mail:

Employment Information

Employer:

Job Title:

Parent 2 Information—   Circle   Mother   Father

Name (Last, First, MI):

Date of Birth:	Age:	Sex:

Current Address:

City:	State:	Zip Code:

Telephone and E-mail Contact Information

Home:	Work:	Cell:

E-mail:

Employment Information

Employer:

Job Title:

Siblings

Name	Natural / Step	Age	Grade	School

Other Household Members

Name	Age	Relationship to Child

Abbreviated Medical History

Child's Primary-Care Physician's Name and Contact Information:

Health Problems:

Medications:

Previous or Current Counseling:

Psychiatric Hospitalizations:

Additional Information

Payment Arrangements

Fee per Session:

Method of Payment:

Insurance Coverage:

Therapist:

AIMS PILOT PROJECT
RELEASE OF INFORMATION

AUTHORIZATION TO RELEASE/REQUEST INFORMATION

I, _____ , born _____ ,
hereby authorize the AIMS team and my therapist to release, request, and share information
regarding my therapy in the AIMS program.

The names of the persons included in this release are:

_____

_____

_____

The court included in this release is: _____

_____   _____
Signature of client   Witnessed by

_____   _____
Date of signature   Witness relationship to client

If the client is a minor (under the age of eighteen), this release must be signed by the client's
parent or legal guardian.

_____   _____
Parent or legal guardian   Relationship to client

ACKNOWLEDGMENTS

A traditional Irish saying goes, "Get down on your knees and thank God you're still on your feet." While working full-time, writing a book, running a business, and attending to family and life, I often whisper this prayer. Although what humbles me immediately is my awareness and deep appreciation of the people who have supported, helped, and been there during this journey. Thanking people from one's very foundation is hard because you know you are imperfect, and gratitude is difficult using the limitations of the written word.

I start with family. When you had to understand that I wouldn't always be there due to the pressure of writing and deadlines, it took special strength as a family to support. I give you, my children and grand angels, huge thanks for understanding and supporting this project. I have dedicated the book to you. I love you all more than words could ever begin to express.

Susan Schulman, agent: My respect and appreciation for you runs deep. Your professionalism, honesty, hard work, incredible integrity, kindness, responsiveness, and most of all your belief in my projects will never be forgotten. You are always there. You truly hear. You understand. I am deeply grateful to have worked with you and your agency. Special thanks to Linda Migalti, rights director for Susan Schulman: A Literary Agency. Linda, you have been amazing working with foreign translations and international agents.

Leslie Meredith, senior editor at Atria: My deep gratitude, Leslie. I know how hard you worked on this book. Thank you for your incredible expertise, valuable time, and your belief in my projects. It was a true blessing to work with you again.

Donna Loffredo, associate editor at Atria: Your kindness and patience is indeed appreciated! I still hear your warm smile over the phone lines.

The staff at Atria: A special thanks for the final phases and hard work. The details in the end . . . brilliant and respectful!

Deborah Griesbach, freelance editor: I'm convinced that Susan had some intuitive feeling when she introduced us. To have worked all these days, weeks, and months together without a glitch is more than amazing to me. You came to this project without ego. You said from the beginning that your goal was to hear me on every level and to help me express my ideas in my own voice. You were never afraid to say if you didn't get something and always took the time to understand. Your calm and encouraging nature was a gift that I appreciated immensely on the frenzied days. I guess that was your volunteer EMT persona kicking into action! Your intelligence and adventuresome spirit kept this book alive. Thank you, Deborah. Thank you.

Danelle Morton, freelance editor: Your step in at the final run was amazing, fast, intelligent, and supportive. I especially appreciated your positive spirit, sense of humor, and kindness. Thank you for hearing me on important issues for this book.

Valerie Martinez: How I found such an angel for an executive assistant is beyond me. You have been wonderful to work with and are an exemplar of kindness. I cannot thank you enough for all your hard work, support, and timely projects. Your expertise and research in finding resources for children in the bibliography was a gift that will keep on giving.

Chris Kitzmiller: We've seen some years together. My friend, you are amazing. I so respect the expertise you have in Web design and social media. I'm grateful that you can translate what I want into techno-speak! My respect for you and your many talents has continued to grow over the years, and I want you to know how much I value you. Thanks and more thanks.

Jennifer Moore-Evans, computer guru from Radian Group: To have to switch to a new computer system, transfer data, and refigure an entire office while writing a book could not have been done without you. You were great. Not to mention your cheerleading for the book, flexibility, and great attitude when my computer skills needed upgrading. You are a special person. Thanks so much.

Carolina Dilullo: You, my dear, a great friend and wonderful help during this busy time. Such energy and gusto you have. You helped keep the many balls in the air from home to office. You were always there with a smile and your great laugh. Your support and help is so appreciated.

Joseph Becker, better known as Spanky: Thanks, Spanky, for all the help at the office and your great attitude when we needed things fast and furious. Which seemed to happen a lot!

Kate Alexander, LCSW, therapy associate: Kate, you are a gift to children. You have that special talent of connecting to little ones, and they feel your love. The healing transformations we have seen in our young clients with your help is nothing short of amazing. You have also been a great friend, colleague, and cheerleader. You are a dear person and I appreciate, love, and honor you. Thank you.

Claudia and Ed Alexander: Thanks to you both for all the support and help you have given over the years as well as for this project. You are both appreciated in many ways. Your kindness feels like a second family to me. How can I say thanks for that? It means the world. Claudia, special thanks for reading the book in rough draft and for your many wonderful suggestions. I will always remember your being there in the end run.

Peg Blackmore: Once again, I say thanks to you for your maternal kindness and blanket understanding. You are such a lovely person and have always been there.

Professional colleagues Dr. Renee Richker, Allison Brittsan, Chris Radeff: Asking you to take the time from your busy schedules to be readers was a lot to request. You all honored the project with your time, support, and expertise. I am more than grateful for your professional input.

The team around me for this book was quite incredible. You are all more than special, and my hope is that we will all continue in our own ways to keep helping and advocating for children. Although thanks is hardly enough, I want to say that I have felt blessed having you all on board.

The professionals interviewed for this book deserve a special thanks for taking time out of busy schedules. Dr. Andrew Loizeaux (PRE), David Bolocofsky (family law attorney), Barbara Shindell, LCSW (PRE). Judge Gail Meinster, Magistrate Marianne Marshall Tims, Magistrate Jason Carrithers, John Paul Lyle (family law attorney), Eldon Silverman (attorney), Scott Gelman (attorney), Thurman W. Arnold III (certified family law specialist). Some of you are quoted and others added conceptual knowledge. I also had the opportunity to talk to many other prominent and experienced professionals and judges who spoke to me with great candor but asked to not be quoted or named. I respect that confidentiality. To you all, your expertise and seasoned experience was a tremendous help and is greatly appreciated.

Finally, I want to thank the remarkable interviewees who gave time and emotional energy to share personal and painful stories so that others could be helped. This book could not have been written without you and your spirited and daring courage. While I have changed identifying details, the emotional truth shines through. I heard in the response to my first book that these stories can work transformative miracles in the lives of the people who read them. I am sure I will hear this again. Somewhere out there in this big world some person will read your story and understand in a moment of painful recognition, "That's my life." Other people, struggling to break free of an ensnaring, entangling relationship with a narcissist, will read your stories of healing, transformation, and joy and will grasp in a soaring moment of imagination that they also can be free. Thank you.

Thank you. Thank you. Thank you.

NOTES

CHAPTER 1

1. Michael Friedman, "The So-Called High-Conflict Couple: A Closer Look," *American Journal of Family Therapy* 32, no. 2 (March/April 2004): 101.

2. Sigmund Freud, "On Narcissism: An Introduction," in *The Standard Edition of the Complete Works of Sigmund Freud,* trans. and ed. James Strachey (London: Hogarth Press). vol. 14. (German: "Zur Einführung des Narzißmus.")

3. American Psychiatric Association, *Diagnostic and Statistical Manual of Mental Disorders,* 5th ed. (Arlington, VA: American Psychiatric Association, 2013), 669–70.

4. Ibid., 716.

5. Jean M. Twenge and W. Keith Campbell, *The Narcissism Epidemic: Living in the Age of Entitlement* (New York: Atria Books, 2010), 2.

6. Mark Gouldston, "Just Listen—Don't Confuse a Narcissist with Asperger's Syndrome," Huffpost Healthy Living, http://www.huffingtonpost.com/mark-goulston-md/just-listen—dont-confus_b_316169.html.

7. http://www.amazon.com/Smead-Hanging-Folder-Letter-64062/product-reviews/B0006VNIT8.

CHAPTER 2

1. http://www.youtube.com/watch?v=tbvVvZls3PA&feature=youtube.

2. Karyl McBride, *Will I Ever Be Good Enough? Healing the Daughters of Narcissistic Mothers* (New York: Simon & Schuster, 2008), 18–35.

3. Ibid., adapted from checklist on 214.

4. Rainer Maria Rilke, *Letters to a Young Poet*, trans. Stephen Mitchell (New York: Vintage, 1986), 68.

CHAPTER 3

1. Jim Butcher, *Turn Coat*, large print ed. (Detroit: Thorndike Press, 2009), 261–62.

CHAPTER 4

1. Robert McAfee Brown, ed., *The Essential Reinhold Niebuhr: Selected Essays and Addresses* (New Haven, CT: Yale University Press, 1987), 251.

2. Stephanie Donaldson-Pressman and Robert M. Pressman, *The Narcissistic Family: Diagnosis and Treatment* (San Francisco: Jossey-Bass, 1997), 18.

3. Audio interview with Dr. Gordon Livingston, author of *How to Love*, http://www.willieverbegoodenough.com/resources/good-enough -rocks-radio-archive/.

4. Donaldson-Pressman and Pressman, *The Narcissistic Family*, 39.

5. http://abclocal.go.com/wabc/story?section=news/local/new_ york&id=9369152.

CHAPTER 5

1. Michael Friedman, "The So-Called High-Conflict Couple: A Closer Look," *American Journal of Family Therapy* 32, no. 2 (March/April 2004): 103.

2. American Psychiatric Association, *Diagnostic and Statistical Manual of Mental Disorders*, 5th ed. (Arlington, VA: American Psychiatric Association, 2013), 671.

3. Anonymous response to Dr. Karyl McBride's *Psychology Today* blog article "Help! I'm Divorcing a Narcissist," http://www .psychologytoday.com/blog/the-legacy-distorted-love/201203/help-im -divorcing-narcissist/comments. The original article was published March 29, 2012, and this comment was posted on September 10, 2013.

CHAPTER 6

1. "DIY Divorce: Why You Should Think Twice before Divorcing without a Lawyer," *Huffington Post*, August 14, 2013, http://www .huffingtonpost.com/2013/08/14/diy-divorce-n_3756900.html.

2. Kendra Randall Jolivet, "The Psychological Impact of Divorce on Children: What Is a Family Lawyer to Do?" *American Journal of Family Law* 25, no. 4 (Winter 2012): 181.

3. Thurman W. Arnold III, "Beware of Lawyers Who Advertise 'Aggressive Divorce,'" CuttingEdgeLaw.com, January 31, 2010, http://cuttingedgelaw.com/blog/beware-lawyers-who-advertise-aggressive-divorce-clients-can-bring-about-paradigm-shift. Attorney Arnold's blog can be found at http://www.EnlightenedDivorceBlog.com.

4. Nicole Black, "Unbundled Legal Services: Steph Kimbro Tells You Everything You Need to Know," MyCase, February 26, 2013, http://www.mycase.com/blog/2013/02/unbundled-legal-services-steph-kimbro-tells-you-everything-you-need-to-know/.

5. http://www.thefreedictionary.com/mediation.

6. Thurman W. Arnold III, "Secrets of Peacemaking: Understanding-Based Guides for Opening a Dialogue with Our Inner Selves," CuttingEdgeLaw.com, February 22, 2011, http://cuttingedgelaw.com/content/secrets-peacemaking-understanding-basedguides-opening-dialogue-our-inner-selves.

7. Colorado Revised Statutes, C.R.S. 14-10-124, "Best Interests of Child," http://www.lexisnexis.com/hottopics/colorado/?app=00075&view=full&interface=1&docinfo=off&searchtype=get&search=C.R.S.+14-10-124.

CHAPTER 7

1. American Psychiatric Association, *Diagnostic and Statistical Manual of Mental Disorders*, 5th ed. (Arlington, VA: American Psychiatric Association, 2013), 671.

2. Andrew M. Colman, *Oxford Dictionary of Psychology*, 2nd ed. (Oxford, England: Oxford University Press, 2006), 606.

CHAPTER 8

1. This quote is commonly attributed to Frank Sinatra; however, none of the many websites attributing it to him provides a source for it.

2. Elisabeth Kübler-Ross, *On Death and Dying* (New York: Scribner, 1997).

3. Karyl McBride, *Will I Ever Be Good Enough? Healing the Daughters of Narcissistic Mothers* (New York: Simon & Schuster, 2008), adapted from "Questionnaire: Does Your Mother Have Narcissistic Traits?," 15–16.

CHAPTER 9

1. Margery Williams, *The Velveteen Rabbit* (New York: Random House, 1985), 8–9.

2. Frans de Waal, *The Age of Empathy: Nature's Lessons for a Kinder Society* (New York: Harmony Books, 2009), 108.

3. Bruce D. Perry and John Marcellus, "The Impact of Abuse and Neglect on the Developing Brain," Scholastic.com, http://teacher.scholastic.com/professional/bruceperry/abuse_neglect.htm.

4. Roseanna Zhao, "Child Abuse Leaves Epigenetic Marks," National Institutes of Health, National Human Genome Research Institute, https://www.genome.gov/27554258.

5. US Department of Justice, Bureau of Justice Statistics, http://www.statisticbrain.com/domestic-violence-abuse-stats/.

6. Ibid.

7. Melissa M. Stiles, "Witnessing Domestic Violence: The Effect on Children," *American Family Physician* 66, no. 11 (December 1, 2002): 2052–67, http://www.aafp.org/afp/2002/1201/p2052.html.

8. Ibid.

9. Ibid.

10. Joyanna Silberg, "How Many Children Are Court-Ordered into Unsupervised Contact with an Abusive Parent after Divorce?" http://www.leadershipcouncil.org/1/med/PR3.html.

11. Perry and Marcellus, "Impact of Abuse and Neglect."

CHAPTER 10

1. Rebecca Love Kourlis and Dirk Olin, *Rebuilding Justice: Civil Courts in Jeopardy and Why You Should Care* (Golden, CO: Fulcrum Publishing, 2011), 154.

BIBLIOGRAPHY

Ahrons, Constance. *The Good Divorce: Keeping Your Family Together When Your Marriage Comes Apart*. New York: HarperCollins Publishers, 1994.

Baris, Mitchell A., and Carla B. Garrity. *Children of Divorce: A Developmental Approach to Residence and Visitation*. Berkeley, CA: Psytec, 1988.

Baron-Cohen, Simon. *The Science of Evil: On Empathy and the Origins of Cruelty*. Philadelphia, PA: Basic Books, 2012.

Beren, Phyllis, ed. *Narcissistic Disorders in Children and Adolescents: Diagnosis and Treatment*. New York: Jason Aronson, 1998.

Bowlby, John. *A Secure Base: Parent-Child Attachment and Healthy Human Development*. Philadelphia, PA: Basic Books, 1988.

Brown, Byron. *Soul without Shame: A Guide to Liberating Yourself from the Judge Within*. Boston, MA: Shambhala, 1998.

Campbell, W. Keith. *When You Love a Man Who Loves Himself*. Naperville, IL: Sourcebooks Casablanca, 2005.

Cavaiola, Alan, and Neil Lavender. *The One-Way Relationship Workbook: Step-by-Step Help for Coping with Narcissists, Egotistical Lovers, Toxic Coworkers & Others Who Are Incredibly Self-Absorbed*. Oakland, CA: New Harbinger Publications, 2011.

Donaldson-Pressman, Stephanie, and Robert M. Pressman. *The Narcissistic Family: Diagnosis and Treatment*. San Francisco, CA: Jossey-Bass, 1997.

Fisher, Bruce, and Robert Alberti. *Rebuilding When Your Relationship Ends*. 3rd ed. Atascadero, CA: Impact Publishers, 2005.

Friedman, Michael. "The So-Called High-Conflict Couple: A Closer Look." *American Journal of Family Therapy* 32, no. 2 (March/April 2004).

Lerner, Rokelle. *The Object of My Affection Is in My Reflection: Coping with Narcissists*. Deerfield Beach, FL: HCI Books, 2008.

Lowrance, Michele. *The Good Karma Divorce: Avoid Litigation, Turn Negative Emotions into Positive Actions, and Get On with the Rest of Your Life.* New York: HarperOne, 2010.

McBride, Karyl. *Will I Ever Be Good Enough? Healing the Daughters of Narcissistic Mothers.* New York: Simon & Schuster, 2008.

Paul, Jordan, and Margaret Paul. *Do I Have to Give Up Me to Be Loved by You.* 2nd ed. Center City, MN: Hazelden, 2002.

Richardson, Pamela. *A Kidnapped Mind: A Mother's Heartbreaking Memoir of Parental Alienation Syndrome.* Toronto, Canada: Dundurn Press, 2006.

Secunda, Victoria. *When Madness Comes Home: Help and Hope for Families of the Mentally Ill.* New York: Hyperion Books, 1998.

Solomon, Marion. *Narcissism and Intimacy: Love and Marriage in an Age of Confusion.* New York: W. W. Norton, 1989.

Sulston, John, and Georgina Ferry. *The Common Thread: A Story of Science, Politics, Ethics and the Human Genome.* London: Joseph Henry Press Books, 2002.

Swithin, Tina, and Carole Lieberman. *Divorcing a Narcissist: One Mom's Battle.* Seattle, WA: Create Space, 2012.

Szalavitz, Maia, and Bruce D. Perry. *Born for Love: Why Empathy Is Essential—and Endangered.* New York: William Morrow, 2010.

Warshak, Richard A. *Divorce Poison New and Updated Edition: How to Protect Your Family from Bad-Mouthing and Brainwashing.* New York: William Morrow, 2010.

Whiteman, Thomas. *Innocent Victims: How to Help Your Children Overcome the Trauma of Divorce* (The Fresh Start Series). Nashville, TN: Thomas Nelson, 1993.

Yudofsky, Stuart C. *Fatal Flaws: Navigating Destructive Relationships with People with Disorders of Personality and Character.* Washington, DC: American Psychiatric Publishing, 2007.

EMPATHY RESOURCES

INTERNET RESOURCES

Center for Building a Culture of Empathy, http://cultureofempathy.com.

BOOKS ABOUT EMPATHY

Decety, Jean, and William Ickes. *The Social Neuroscience of Empathy*. Cambridge, MA: MIT Press, 2011.

de Waal, Frans. *The Age of Empathy: Nature's Lessons for a Kinder Society*. New York: Broadway Books, 2010.

Iacoboni, Marco. *Mirroring People: The Science of Empathy and How We Connect with Others*. New York: Farrar, Straus & Giroux, 2008.

Szalavitz, Maia, and Bruce D. Perry. *Born for Love: Why Empathy Is Essential—and Endangered*. New York: William Morrow, 2010.

BOOKS ABOUT PARENTING WITH EMPATHY

Faber, Adele, and Elaine Mazlish. *How to Talk So Kids Will Listen & Listen So Kids Will Talk*. Updated edition. New York: Scribner, 2012.

Gottman, John, with Joan Declaire. *Raising an Emotionally Intelligent Child: The Heart of Parenting*. New York: Simon & Schuster, 1998.

Hall, Karyn D., and Melissa H. Cook. *The Power of Validation: Arming Your Child Against Bullying, Peer Pressure, Addiction, Self-Harm, and Out-of-Control Emotions*. Oakland, CA: New Harbinger, 2011.

Walfish, Fran. *The Self-Aware Parent: Resolving Conflict and Building a Better Bond with Your Child*. New York: Palgrave Macmillan, 2010.

RESOURCES FOR CHILDREN

DIVORCE

Bruno, Ellen. *SPLIT: A Film for Kids of Divorce (and Their Parents)*. *SPLIT* can be ordered from its website, www.splitfilm.org. This film was made in collaboration with children aged 6–12.

Buscemi, Karen. *Split in Two: Keeping It Together When Your Parents Live Apart*. San Francisco, CA: Zest Books, 2009. Age range: 11–17 years.

Evans, Joshua, and his stepmother. *How to Go to Visitation without Throwing Up*. Livingston, TX: Pale Horse Publishing, 2002. Age range: 7–13 years.

Holyoke, Nancy, and Scott Nash (illustrator). *A Smart Girl's Guide to Her Parents' Divorce: How to Land on Your Feet When Your World Turns Upside Down*. Middleton, WI: American Girl Publishing, 2009. Age range: 9 and up.

Levins, Sandra, and Bryan Langdo. *Was It the Chocolate Pudding?: A Story for Little Kids about Divorce*. Washington, DC: Magination Press, 2006. Age range: 4 and up.

Lowry, Danielle, and Bonnie and Ellen Candace (illustrators). *What Can I Do?: A Book for Children of Divorce*. Washington, DC: Magination Press, 2002. Age range: 9 and up.

MacGregor, Cynthia. *The Divorce Helpbook for Teens*. Atascadero, CA: Impact Publishers, 2004. Age range: teenagers.

Masurel, Claire, and Kady MacDonald Denton (illustrator). *Two Homes*. Somerville, MA: Candlewick, 2003. Age range: 3–7 years.

Moore-Mallinos, Jennifer, and Marta Fabrega, (illustrator). *When My Parents Forgot How to Be Friends*. Hauppauge, NY: Barron's Educational Series, 2005. Age range: 4–7 years.

Schmitz, Tamara. *Standing on My Own Two Feet: A Child's Affirmation of Love in the Midst of Divorce*. New York: Price Stern Sloan, 2008. Age range: 3–7 years.

Stern, Zoe, and Evan Stern (with a little help from their mom, Ellen Sue Stern). *Divorce Is Not the End of the World: Zoe and Evan's Coping Guide for Kids*. Berkeley, CA: Tricycle Press, 2008. Age range: 8–12 years.

Thomas, Pat. *My Family's Changing*. Hauppauge, NY: Barron's Educational Series, 1999. Age range: 4 and up.

Winchester, Kent, and Roberta Beyer. *What in the World Do You Do When Your Parents Divorce?: A Survival Guide for Kids*. Minneapolis, MN: Free Spirit Publishing, 2001. Age range: 7–12 years.

EMOTIONS

Cain, Janan. *The Way I Feel*. Seattle, WA: Parenting Press, 2000. Age range: 3–8 years.

Doleski, Teddi, and William Hart McNichols (illustrator). *The Hurt*. Mahwah, NJ: Paulist Press, 1983. Age range: 5 and up.

Goldblatt, Rob. *The Boy Who Didn't Want to Be Sad*. Washington, DC: Magination Press, 2004. Age range: 4 and up.

Holmes, Margaret M., Sasha J. Mudlaff, and Cary Pillo (illustrator). *A Terrible Thing Happened*. Washington, DC: Magination Press, 2000. Age range: 4 and up.

Karst, Patrice, and Geoff Stevenson (illustrator). *The Invisible String*. Camarillo, CA: DeVorss, 2000. Age range: 3 and up.

McCloud, Carol, and David Messing (illustrator). *Have You Filled a Bucket Today?: A Guide to Daily Happiness for Kids*. Northville, MI: Ferne Press, 2006. Age range: 4–8 years.

Nemiroff, Marc, Jane Annunziata, and Christine Battuz (illustrator). *Shy Spaghetti and Excited Eggs: A Kid's Menu of Feelings*. Washington, DC: Magination Press, 2011. Age range: 5 and up.

Sornson, Bob, and Shelley Johannes (illustrator). *Stand in My Shoes: Kids Learning about Empathy*. Golden, CO: Love and Logic Press, 2013. Age range: 5 and up.

Williams, Margery. *The Velveteen Rabbit*. New York: Random House, 1985.

Wolff, Ferida, Harriet May Savitz, and Marie LeTourneau (illustrator). *Is a Worry Worrying You?* Terre Haute, IN: Tanglewood Press, 2005. Age range: 4–8 years.

ABUSE

Bernstein, Sharon Chesler, and Karen Ritz (illustrator). *A Family That Fights*. Morton Grove, IL: Albert Whitman, 1991. Age range: 5–9 years.

Davis, Diane. *Something Is Wrong at My House: A Book about Parents' Fighting*. Seattle, WA: Parenting Press, 1984. Age range: 3–8 years.

Lee, Ilene, Kathy Sylwester, and Carol Deach (illustrator). *When Mommy Got Hurt: A Story for Young Children about Domestic Violence*. Oakland, CA: Storymine Press, 2011. Age range: 2–7 years.

Loftis, Chris, and Catharine Gallagher (illustrator). *The Words Hurt: Helping Children Cope with Verbal Abuse*. Far Hills, NJ: New Horizon Press, 1997. Age range: 4–8 years.

Sanders, Jayneen, and Craig Smith (illustrator). *Some Secrets Should Never Be Kept*. Victoria, Australia: UpLoad Publishing, 2013. Age range: 3–12 years.

Trottier, Maxine, and Judith Friedman (illustrator). *A Safe Place*. Park Ridge, IL: Albert Whitman, 1997. Age range: 5–8 years.

Watts, Gillian, and Ben Hodson (illustrator). *Hear My Roar: A Story of Family Violence*. Buffalo, NY: Annick Press, 2009. Age range: 5–7 years.

Winn, Christine M. (author/illustrator), and David Walsh *Clover's Secret*. Minneapolis, MN: Fairview Press, 1996. Age range: 4–8 years.

SUBSTANCE ABUSE

Anonymous. *The 12 Steps Unplugged: A Young Person's Guide to Alcoholics Anonymous*. Center City, MN: Hazelden, 2003. Age range: teens.

Auth, Jeannine. *Emmy's Question*. St. Augustine, FL: Morningtide Press, 2007. Ages 7 and up.

Bakewell, Lisa. *Alcohol Information for Teens: Health Tips about Alcohol and Alcoholism*. Detroit, MI: Omnigraphics, 2009. Age range: Teens.

Heegaard, Marge. *When a Family Is in Trouble: Children Can Cope with Grief from Drug and Alcohol Addiction*. Chapmanville, WV: Woodland Press, 1996. Age range: 9 and up.

Leib Higgins, Pamela, and Gail Zawacki (illustrator). *Up and Down the Mountain: Helping Children Cope with Parental Alcoholism*. Far Hills, NJ: New Horizon Press, 1994. Age range: 4–8 years.

American Beauty, 1999 (Sam Mendes)

Baby Boom, 1987 (Charles Shyer)

Beaches, 1988 (Garry Marshall)

Beauty and the Beast, 1991 (Walt Disney Feature Animation)

Because I Said So, 2007 (Michael Lehmann)

Beethoven's 2nd, 1993 (Rod Daniel)

Dear Zachary, 2008 (Heidi Ewing, Rachel Grady)

The Devil Wears Prada, 2006 (David Frankel)

Divine Secrets of the Ya Ya Sisterhood, 2002 (Callie Khouri)

East of Eden, 1955 (Elia Kazan)

Emperor's New Groove, 2000 (Walt Disney Feature Animation)

Empire Falls, 2005 (Fred Schepis)

Enough, 2002 (Michael Apted)

Ever After: A Cinderella Story, 1998 (Bobby Farrelly, Peter Farrelly)

Georgia Rule, 2007 (Garry Marshall)

Gia, 1998 (Michael LeRoy)

Girl, Interrupted, 1999 (James Mangold)

Gypsy, 1962 (Mervyn LeRoy)

Intolerable Cruelty, 2003 (Joel Coen, Ethan Coen)

The Joy Luck Club, 1993 (Wayne Wang)

Kramer vs. Kramer, 1979 (Robert Benton)

Life or Something Like It, 2002 (Stephen Herek)

The Little Foxes, 1941 (William Wyler)

Matilda, 1996 (Danny DeVito)

Mermaids, 1990 (Richard Benjamin)

Miss Potter, 2006 (Chris Noonan)

Mommie Dearest, 1981 (Frank Perry)

Mona Lisa Smile, 2003 (Mike Newell)

Monster-in-Law, 2005 (Robert Luketic)

The Mother, 2003 (Roger Michell)

No Way Out but One, 2011 (Barry Nolan, Garland Waller)

Ordinary People, 1980 (Robert Redford)

The Other Sister, 1999 (Gary Marshall)

The Perfect Man, 2005 (Mark Rosman)

Pieces of April, 2003 (Peter Hedges)

Postcards from the Edge, 1990 (Mike Nichols)

Precious, 2009 (Lee Daniels)

The Prince of Tides, 1991 (Barbra Streisand)

Prozac Nation, 2003 (Erik Skjoldbjaerg)

Safe Haven, 2013 (David Foenkinos, Stéphane Foenkinos)

The Secret Life of Bees, 2008 (Gina Prince-Bythewood)

Sleeping with the Enemy, 1991 (Joseph Ruben)

Something to Talk About, 1995 (Lasse Hallstrom)

A Streetcar Named Desire, 1951 (Elia Kazan)

Tangled, 2010 (Walt Disney Animation Studios)

Terms of Endearment, 1983 (James L. Brooks)

The War of the Roses, 1989 (Danny DeVito)

What Maisie Knew, 2012 (Scott McGehee, David Siegel)

What's Love Got to Do with It, 1993 (Brian Gibson)

White Oleander, 2002 (Peter Kosminsky)

Young Adult, 2011 (Jason Reitman)

A

ability to love, narcissists' lack of, 10, 51–52, 112–13

admiration, 5, 7–8

AIMS:

case manager assignment, 186, 189, 196

determining success, 192

financial mediator, 192–93

funding of, 191–92

intake forms, 202–6

judicial approval for, 193

maintenance, 190

mission of, 182

as pilot project, 175–82

problems in court system and, 180–81

referral criteria, 183–86

summary of, 193

therapeutic strategies of, 176, 181, 182, 190–91

therapeutic team, 189–90, 191, 196–200

therapy referrals, 186–89

word narcissism not used in, 182–83

Al-Anon, 103

alcoholism, 103, 161

American Psychiatric Association (APA), 5, 6

American Psychological Association, 191

Arnold, Thurman W., III, 90–91, 93

arrogance, 6, 9–10

Asperger's syndrome, 11

assertiveness, 121, 124, 126, 162, 163, 165

attorneys:

adversarial process and, 83–84

"best interest attorneys," 87

collaborative law and, 91, 94

custody and, 67, 89, 169

divorcing a narcissist and, 58, 88, 91–92

evaluation of websites, 86–87

familiarity with narcissism, 88–89

family law attorneys, 83, 86–87, 91, 99

guidelines for hiring, 85–93

initial consultation, 88

initial meetings with, 90–91

interviewing, 88–89

joint decision-making and, 89–90

parenting-time evaluators and, 91, 99, 101

unbundled legal services, 92–93

authentic self, 128, 141–43, 156, 173

B

belief in specialness, 5, 7

body image, 22

ABOUT THE AUTHOR

Karyl McBride, Ph.D., LMFT, is a licensed marriage and family therapist in Denver, Colorado, with thirty-four years of public and private practice. She specializes in treating couples, families, children, and individuals with dysfunctional-family issues, as well as trauma and divorce. For the past twenty-plus years, Dr. McBride has been researching narcissism in intimate relationships. She is a leading authority on the topic of narcissism and is the author of *Will I Ever Be Good Enough? Healing the Daughters of Narcissistic Mothers*, published in 2008.

Dr. McBride's private practice is diverse, with specialties in the treatment of sexual abuse, victimization issues, marriage and relationship problems, codependency, divorce, stepfamilies, sexual-abuse clinical assessments, and assessment and treatment for children who sexually act out. She also provides forensic consulting and has testified as an expert witness in eighty-six trials. She was asked to present her doctoral work at an international police research conference in Ljubljana, Slovenia, in 1996.

Dr. McBride's work has been featured in numerous magazines and newspapers and on websites, radio shows, and television, including *Dr. Phil*, HLN, *Elle*, *Cleo*, and *Maclean's*. She is a contributing blogger for online *Psychology Today*. More information can be found on her two websites: www.willieverbegoodenough.com and www.karylmcbridephd.com. She can also be found on social media such as Facebook (https://www.facebook.com/DrKarylMcBride), as well as LinkedIn, and Twitter.

To contact Dr. McBride for speaking engagements, media, workshops, or further information, e-mail her at dr.mcbride@att.net.